There are five titles in the 'Get Going With Creative Writing' series:

All About Me – 978-1-907733-90-1

Likes and Dislikes – 978-1-907733-91-8

Out and About – 978-1-907733-92-5

We Love Animals – 978-1-907733-93-2

What We Do – 978-1-907733-94-9

Guinea Pig Education
2 Cobs Way
New Haw, Addlestone
Surrey
KT15 3AF
Tel: 01932 336553
Website: www.guineapigeducation.co.uk

© Copyright 2014

NO part of this publication may be reproduced, stored or copied for commercial purposes and profit without the prior written permission of the publishers.

ISBN: 978-1-907733-92-5

Written: Sally A Jones and Amanda C Jones
Illustrations: Sally A Jones
Graphic Design: Annalisa Jones
USA Editing: S. Waller

Dear Kids,

Have fun learning to write with our 'Get Going With Creative Writing' series. Enjoy reading our short stories; some of which have been written by kids your age. Use our ideas to write your own stories, or try some non-fiction writing, such as, diaries, reports and leaflets. If you read or write well you will achieve high grades at school, so we challenge you to learn to love writing. You just need a notebook and pencil to start working through your guinea pig writing guide. Don't forget to color in the pictures.

Dear Teachers and Parents,

If your children think writing is dull, give them a guinea pig writing book from the 'Get Going With Creative Writing' series and we think they'll change their minds. However, these books are also ideal for those children who love to write, providing starting points that will make any budding young writer's imagination run wild, especially if they are preparing for standardized tests.

We have put together a series of themed books to inspire your child to write at his or her level. Whether you choose 'About Me,' 'We Love Animals,' 'Likes and Dislikes,' 'Out And About' or 'What We Do,' you will choose an English study book with a light-hearted, modern approach to appeal to the children of today.

The books can be used at home or in school alongside the existing curriculum. Inside, you will find a treasure trove of ideas for writing, featuring fiction and non-fiction themes. Based on the National Curriculum in the UK, they use respected strategies for literacy, with tips on planning and writing techniques, sentence construction, grammar tips and more.

Written by a former teacher, working as a tutor, the books have been tested by the children the author teaches in Surrey, England. These children agree the books are fun and help them learn to love writing.

> We would like to thank the students of Guinea Pig Tuition – class of 2010/2011 – Sophia, Georgina, Harriet, Hannah, Sacha, Harry, Gareth, Rahan, Neena, Mahir, Neesha, Jai, Alexandra, Anna Maria and Vlad.

Write the story by choosing a suitable ending for each sentence.

Paragraph 1

For his birthday Elliot received a new kite. It was not just an ordinary kite, but a stunt kite that...

- did acrobatics in the air.
- did loops and dives.
- flew like a bird or dragon.
- ....
- ....

As soon as Grandma cleared away the breakfast, Elliot and his sister Kate ...

- *fetched the kite from Dad's car trunk.*
- *took the kite out of its packet.*
- *read the instructions carefully.*
- ....

Then Grandpa and Elliot ...

- *made up the stunt kite.*
- *put the pieces together.*
- *assembled the parts.*
- ....

They planned to try out the new kite ...

- *in the park.*
- *on the top of the cliffs.*
- *on the beach.*

Paragraph 2

As they set out ...

- *the wind blew strongly.*
- *the sun shone brightly.*
- *a breeze blew gently.*

"Get ready for the launch," Elliot shouted...

- *excitedly.*
- *enthusiastically.*
- *wildly.*
- ....

As he let go, the kite ...

- *soared high in the sky.*
- *rose up in the air.*
- *flapped its tail in the wind.*
- ....

"This is great," he squealed ...

- *in excitement.*
- *joyfully.*
- *happily.*
- ....

"Let me hold it," whined Kate ...

- *grabbing*
- *seizing hold of*
- *snatching*
- ....

the kite's controls.

"Stop it," hissed Elliot ...

- *"It's mine."*
- *"It's my birthday present."*
- *"You can have a turn later on."*
- ....

In the tussle, Elliot let go. He ...

- *gasped,*
- *cried out,*
- *screamed,*
- *...............,*

"Look what you've made me do."

The family watched the kite ...

- *sail away,*
- *fly high into the sky,*
- *dance in the clouds,*
- *............................*

but then it ...

- *crashed down,*
- *fell fast,*
- *dived towards the ground,*
- *............................*

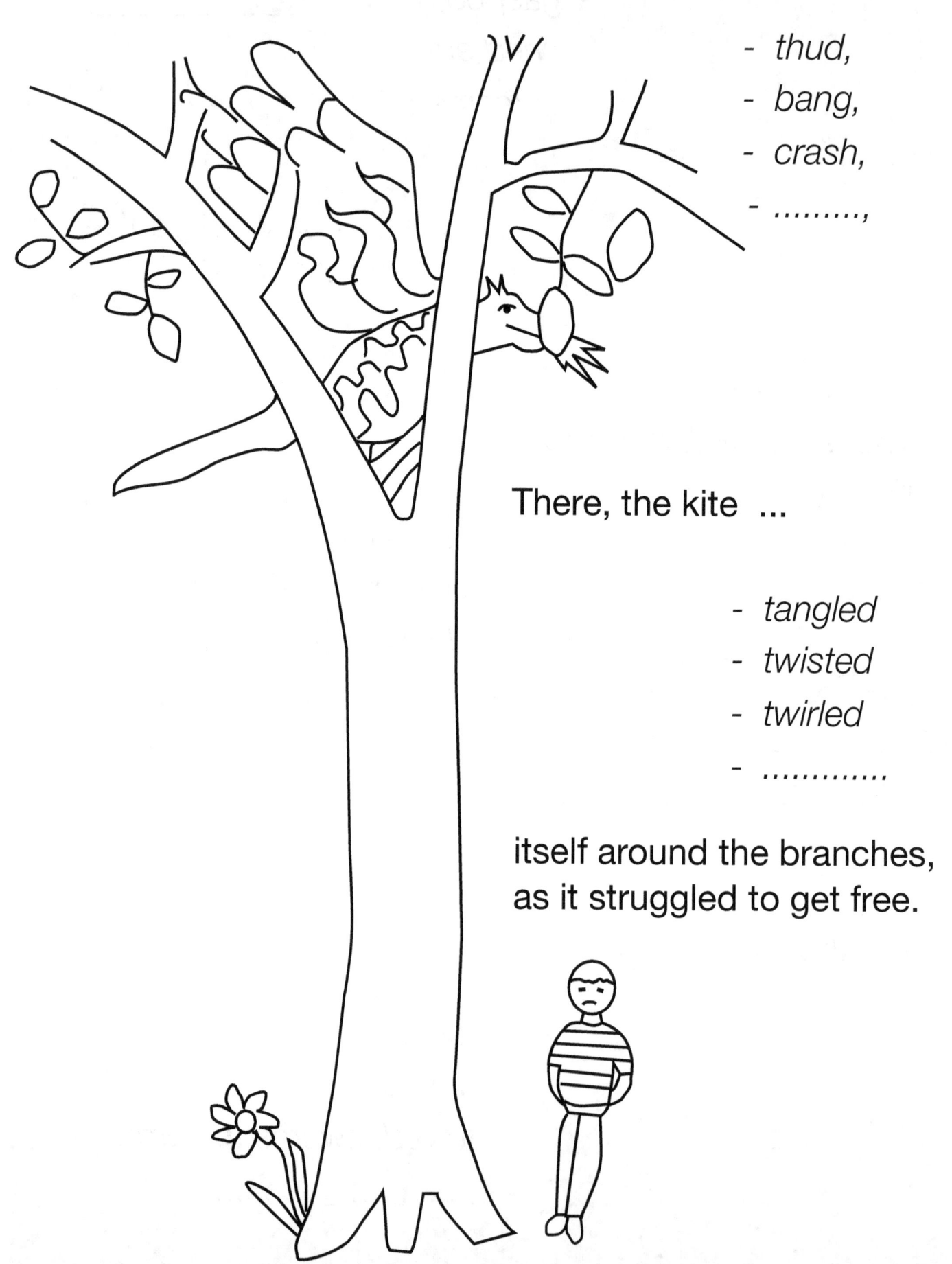

Paragraph 3

Below, the family ...

- *poked at the tree trunk*
- *threw sticks into the branches*
- *shook the tree*
- ...., to get it out.

It ...

- *would not budge.*
- *was stuck tight.*
- *was entwined in the branches.*
- ....

Elliot tried to climb the tree, but it was ...

- *too tall.*
- *too dangerous.*
- *too difficult.*
- ....

The kite stared down at them ...

- *like a wounded bird.*
- *like a broken toy.*
- ....

Elliot felt ...
- *tearful,*
- *sad,*
- *remorseful,*
- *................,*

at the loss of his new toy stunt kite.

That is where the kite stayed for months and months ...
- *battered by the sea wind.*
- *shredded by the gales.*
- *being a companion to the birds.*
- *..*

However, Grandma and Grandpa were always there for Elliot and bought him ...

- *a bigger and better stunt kite,*
- *a designer kite,*
- *a replacement,*

which he flew every time the wind blew.

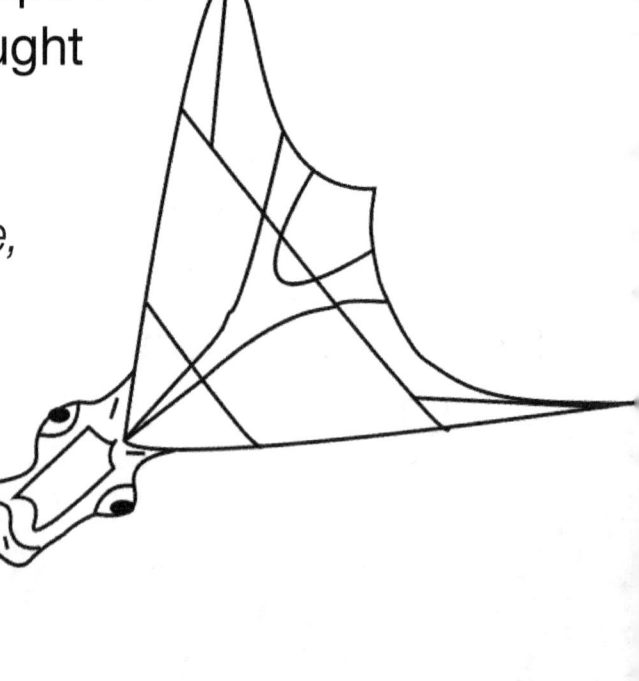

Let's write a stunt kite story. Can you think of some ideas?

The <u>starting point</u> of your story is the <u>first sentence</u>:

> For my birthday I received a kite. It was not just an ordinary kite, but a stunt kite in the shape of a ...

You must decide if your story is going to be a realistic one, or it may be that it is a magic kite that takes you on a fantastic adventure to a faraway place. It may be a modern fairytale or a fantasy, where weird and wonderful things happen or where good overcomes evil.

Let's plan the story

Jot down a few of your own ideas.

The characters are:	The setting is:	The plot is:
•me, my grandpa (for example)	•the park on top of the cliffs near the home of my grandparents.	•about a new kite that flies away.

Paragraph 1: The Story Begins

Introduce the characters, the setting and start the plot:

- I build my new stunt kite.
- It is in the shape of a fierce dragon.
- Grandpa and I fly it on top of the cliffs.

Paragraph 2: Develop the plot

What might happen to trigger a series of events:

- I launch the kite, but the stong wind pulls it.
- I can hardly hold on... but I WILL NOT LET GO.
- A strong wind lifts me up, up, up into the sky.
- I am flying on my magic kite, on the end of the kite's string.
- I feel terror and fear.

Paragraph 3: How will the story end?

Wind up the story with a suitable resolution.

I'm lifted up with my kite on the wind. I sail through the clouds holding tightly onto my kite's string.

Choose one of these endings:

1. I can't hold on. I fall into the sea, but I'm rescued by a boat.
2. I am flown to a faraway place in the sky, where I meet the citizens of a strange bouncy country. The King and Queen welcome me and I become famous.
3. My dragon kite meets a monster kite and they fight for territory. A great bird rescues me and takes me on his wings back home.

1. **A RESCUE story**
2. **An ADVENTURE story**
3. **A FANTASY story**

Will I tell my story:

- in **first person**, so I am the main character telling the story (using I or we).

- in the **third person** (using he or she).

Now, think of some good vocabulary you can use in your story.

Stunt kites can be shaped like monsters or dragons because they:

- soar and sail
- turn and twist
- fly off alone
- struggle
- entwine
- tear/rip

- dive and dip
- flutter in the breeze
- crash down
- tangle
- fight
- snarl

- ride the air currents
- sail away
- get stuck in a tree
- flap
- gnash their teeth
- battle

Write a story called:

The Stunt Kite

Before you start writing, read the story below.
Which ending do you like best?

For my birthday I received a kite. It was not just an ordinary kite, but a stunt kite in the shape of a dragon.

Before Grandpa asked, I knew what I wanted to do that day. I wanted to make up my kite. Together, we tore off the outer packaging and then followed the instructions to assemble the parts. In less than ten minutes, the stunt kite was ready to fly. We decided to try it out immediately so we walked down the steep hill that led to the grassy park on the cliff top. I clutched the stunt kite under my arm; the dragon face fixed its gaze on me. He had two black pools for eyes and flaming red nostrils. Would he fly well, I wondered?

On our arrival at the park, the wind was blowing fiercely but we carefully untangled the strings and prepared for take off. Then I launched my kite, WHOOSH! It soared high into the sky. Grandpa watched as I ran with the kite. It dipped and dived above us in the sky. Suddenly, there was a mighty gust of wind, which wrenched at the kite strings. I did not let go and I was lifted up into the air. "Grandpa," I cried out. "Help me! Help me!" Grandpa just stood looking dumbfounded.

Which ending?

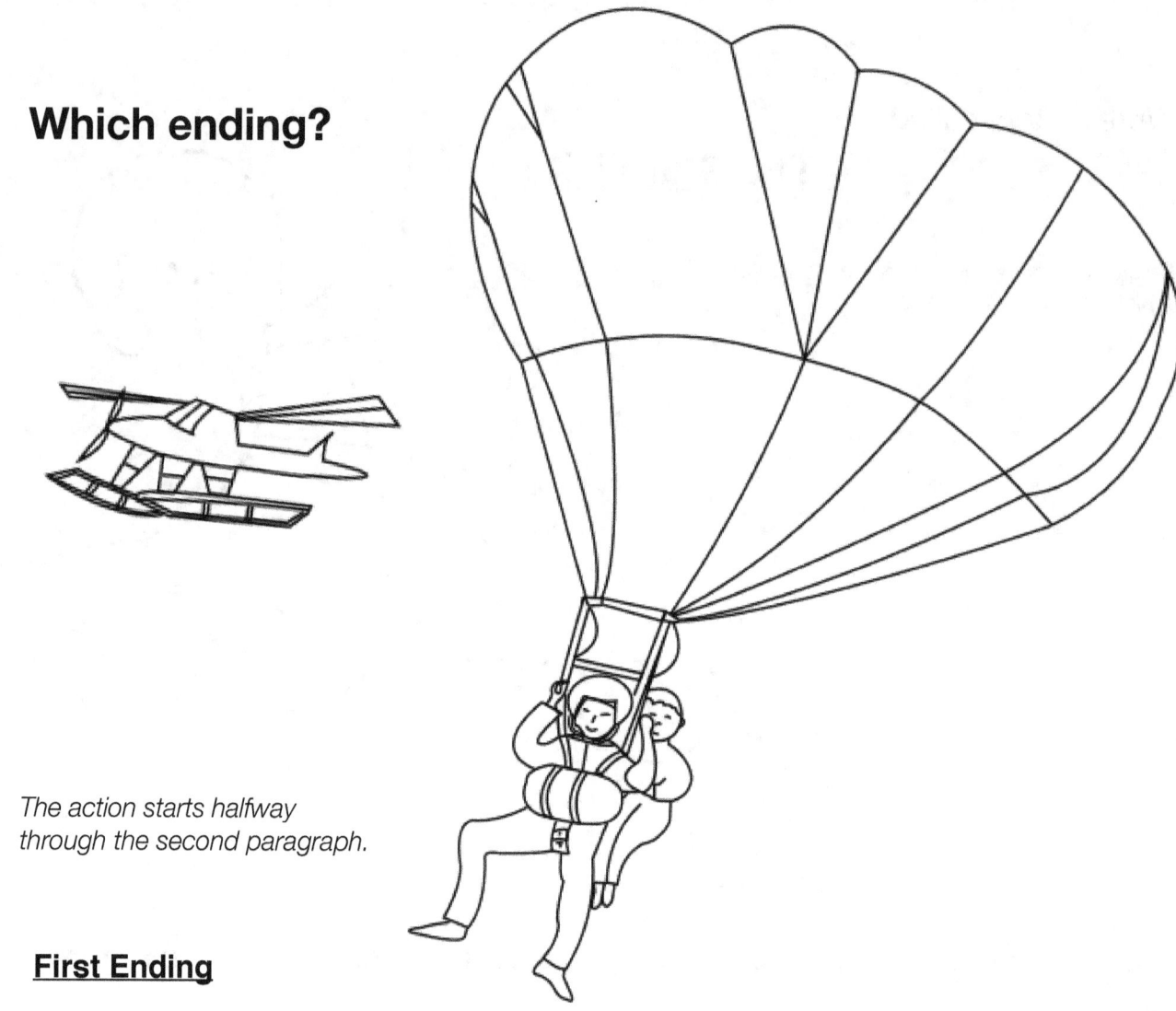

The action starts halfway through the second paragraph.

First Ending

I clung to the kite string desperately. I was flying with the kite across the sky and the people on earth looked like tiny ants.

"Stop," I pleaded to the dragon kite, "take me back to earth," but the kite seemed to ignore my pleas. It was at that moment I let go. I couldn't hold on anymore. I just let go and started to free fall.

"Help me! Someone help me!" I screamed.

It was at that moment I realized that I wasn't alone. A Navy plane was circling below me and skydivers were jumping from the plane one by one. It wasn't long before one of the men spotted me.

"Get on my back," he yelled. I grabbed hold of him and we glided down under his parachute until we landed with a SPLASH in the sea. Then we were hauled into a waiting Navy vessel. The skipper (captain) was astonished to see me but kindly offered to take me back to the shore. As I sat in the boat staring into the bright blue sky, I thought I saw a real dragon heading towards the moon. I've never believed in crazy myths about dragons, but this adventure may have changed my mind.

Second Ending

I clung desperately to the kite string until my knuckles turned white. We traveled across the sky at great speed, flying above the blue sparkling sea. Then we sailed over towns, villages and even mountain ranges which looked like a patchwork quilt below us. We flew in and out of clouds; the journey continued for several hours. Then the stunt kite dragon started to drop down thousands of feet for our descent. Before I knew it, we were gathering speed, getting faster and faster.

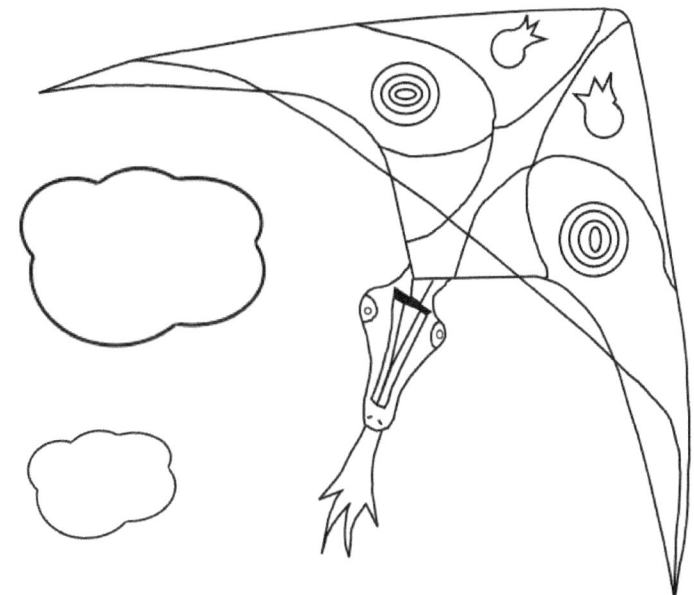

We came down with a thud. My dragon kite landed, but what kind of place was this? As we touched the ground we bounced. I looked cautiously around and I discovered it was a strange bouncy country. The town was a giant trampoline. No one walked. The people jumped and turned somersaults as they greeted us. They hugged my dragon and welcomed him home. Then they bounced over to hug me.

It was then I realized that this was the place where my stunt kite had been made and he had returned today for a big festival. The whole town was in attendance, even the king and queen. They made me a guest of honor because I had come from a land so far away. They showed me the factories where they make fantastic stunt kites, shaped like dragons. I stayed for several days being looked after by the people. Soon it was time to board the plane with the next consignments of stunt kites. As I flew home I thought, these things only happen in fairy tales, but now I'm not so sure.

Third Ending

I clung desperately to the kite string, terrified that I might fall, as we sailed across the sky. Then my heart beat even faster. The sky was getting dark. Everything was going black. We had entered a dark cloud layer and there seemed to be some turbulent weather ahead. Worse than this, there was a terrible roaring sound. Was it thunder? That's when I spied a fearful image out of the corner of my eye. I realized the black cloud was a huge and hideous monster with red eyes and I was heading straight towards him. "Eeek!"

It was as though my dragon kite seemed to have grown larger. He was huge. The dragon kite with black eyes and flaming red nostrils met, head-on, a huge black monster. They snarled at each other, gnashed their teeth and their great bodies tussled. Their mouths gaped open showing a vast row of jagged white teeth and they ripped into each other's flesh until the blood was dripping like rain. I couldn't bear to see my dragon defeated, so I cried out,
"Come on, beat him!" In a split second the monster had turned his attention on me. He was advancing towards me with a menacing look. "Help, help!" I yelled. At that moment an eagle appeared and he snatched me up in his beak, just in the nick of time, so I was saved from the mouth of sharp teeth that threatened to devour me. The bird glided out of the dark cloud, back to the bright blue sky and landed on the grass near my grandpa's house, where Grandpa was waiting to hug me as he wept for joy.
"You know, I never used to believe in all those myths, but now I'm not so sure they're not true."

Story Writing Tips

- Make sure you have an INTERESTING OPENING: "It was not just an ordinary kite but..." This will capture the imagination of the reader and make him or her want to read on.

- In the opening paragraph, introduce believable characters, a setting and a plot. Go straight into the action or use dialogue to move the story on but make it exciting.

- Then, WIND UP YOUR STORY WITH A GOOD ENDING. In the resolution you will have solved all the problems.

- It could be happy, sad, a cliffhanger (which leaves the reader to make up his or her own mind), or a moral ending.

- Have a **memorable final sentence**.

Use a variety of sentences

The dragons fought.

- This is a simple sentence, with a subject and a verb *(fought)*.

The dragons fought ferociously.

- An adverb *(ferociously)* has been added to this sentence.

Up in the black clouds, the fierce dragons fought ferociously.

- This sentence has a subordinate clause (*Up in the black clouds*) and an adjective *(fierce)*.

Up in the black clouds, the fierce dragons fought ferociously, until the blood dripped like rain.

(Until the blood dripped like rain) is a simile and makes the sentence more interesting.

Elliot's teacher asks him to write a poem – it doesn't have to rhyme.
Try writing a poem of your own.

Start each line of a poem with a capital letter.

It's awesome
To watch my stunt kite,
Fly high,
Flapping its
Dragon
Wings in the sky.

From its nostrils,
It breathes out
Fiery flames
And snaps
Its powerful jaw
.... and
Breaks away
From me.

I just stand
And watch it
Soaring higher
And higher.
Roaming the airways,
A dragon -
Wild and free -
No thought of me.

Three hours later,
Tired
And forlorn,
It weaves its
Weary way down,
And falling fast,
Crashes with a BANG
Into a tree.

There -
It's stuck...
In the branches.
A dragon:
Battered and bruised,
Tattered and torn,
Wrestling with the wind.
Struggling to get free;
It looks at me.
What can I do?

Listen Live

Hi, I'm your D.J. George

... and I'm Christabelle

Christabelle, how are you today?

I'm good. How about you, George?

Very good, thank you, Christabelle.

Well, I'm really excited. Our producer has just emailed me to say we're taking the show to Antarctica.

Wow! I've never been there before.

Me neither! We'll be flying out in October.

How long is the flight?

Only eight hours by plane, compared to three weeks by ship. It will be a real adventure.

What's it like out there?

They say it's a desolate, frozen wasteland at the end of the earth. It's the most inhospitable place on earth.

So, where will we stay? Do they have hotels and stores there?

We'll set up studio for one week in one of the scientific research bases. You'll need to take everything, including books, CDs, DVDs, skis, climbing

> gear and lots of spare batteries because there are no stores.
>
> *Oh no! No stores. How will we manage? Looks like I'll have to get out my thermal pants!*
>
> I'll say. I'm taking polar clothing, like a thick padded jacket, so I don't get frostbite. It'll be -22°F or worse... and really windy.
>
> *...You mean, sheep skin insulated boots and fur lined gloves as well. It must be amazing there though. We'll be able to stare into the crystal clear water...*
>
> Yeah. They say that the snow glistens as if it is covered in diamonds. There are ice sculptures and icebergs bigger than cathedrals.
>
> *Will I be able to watch the penguins? I love them. They're my favorite animal.*
>
> Yeah, hundreds of penguins skidding along on their tummies and standing wondering who these strange two legged creatures are in snow suits.
>
> *It'll be awesome. I can't wait.*

What does **dialogue** do?

It tells us what's happening. It gives information about the characters and their relationships with each other.

- This is a radio script, but remember to use "......," "......?" "......!" if you write dialogue in a story.

- Start a new line if a new person speaks.

- Use other words for said: muttered quietly, yelled raucously.

"We have Eric on the line.

Hi Eric. Tell us your exciting story about Norway..."

"The most exciting place I've been to is the frozen North. Uncle Tom and I walked for days across icy snow. It was cold. It was freezing cold, even though the sun was shining. We didn't meet anyone else on our journey.

We camped in a tent for five days. In the evening I built a cave in the snow, just like a polar bear. We had incredible snowball fights. It was such fun. Uncle Tom caught a fish in the icy cold lake and we cooked it on the fire and had it for dinner.

It was thrilling traveling across the snow on a sleigh that was pulled by Husky dogs. We went down a treacherous slope, getting faster, faster, faster."

"That sounds awesome. I don't know about you but I'm starting to feel a bit cold."

"Noah is on the line..."

"WHEN I WAS ON VACATION IN MALAYSIA I SAW A KITE FLYING COMPETITION. THE WINNER WAS THE ONE WHO WENT THE HIGHEST OR STAYED IN THE SKY THE LONGEST TIME. ANOTHER THING, I WALKED THROUGH A TROPICAL RAIN FOREST AND SAW WILD ORCHIDS FLOWERING. I VISITED THE NATIONAL PARK WHERE THEY PROTECT ANIMALS IN DANGER, LIKE LEOPARDS, TIGERS AND RHINOS. IT WAS A GREAT EXPERIENCE."

"Very nice."

"Madison, what's your story?"

"I spent the summer in Istanbul in Turkey. It's a busy city. There are lots of traffic jams on the main roads, but you can take a boat. They travel regularly across the Bosphorus Sea from Europe to Asia or around the islands. The boats are cheap and you can get on and off like you do on a bus.

I saw wonderful sights as I traveled up the Bosphorus on the public boat. I saw the impressive domes of the Hagia Sophia, which has been a church, a mosque and is now a museum. I sailed past the Blue Mosque and the Topkapi Palace.

Then I docked and I took a taxi to the Grand Bazaar, which is a huge shopping center where you can get lost. I haggled with the shop keeper (to get the lowest price) and I bought some bracelets, a bag and a patterned dish. If only I could have brought back a beautiful patterned rug – perhaps next time.

On the pavements I saw dogs snoozing and the sweetest cats with kittens."

"How incredible. I would so love to be there."

George:	"We have Cassey on the line... Hi Cassey. Where's your exciting vacation destination?"
Cassey:	*"It's on the Cote D'Azur in the South of France. I've been going there every year since I was a small child."*
George:	"Yes, that's a wonderful part of the world!"
Cassey:	*"I love to swim in the Mediterranean Sea. The water is so blue, so clear and transparent. I swim up and down amongst the little colored fish. Sometimes I use my snorkel kit and swim under the water watching the marine life. It's fascinating.* *On my last vacation, I saw some local people feeding the fish bread, so the next day I took some bread to feed them. It was amazing because as soon as the bread touched the water, thousands of fish came up to eat it. They came so close to me, even daring to take the bread straight from my hand. I could see all their colors and patterns. One had bright yellow, horizontal stripes and it darted around my legs at lightning speed. The experience made me realize that fish are more intelligent than I gave them credit for being.* *Anyway, I became so interested in the marine life in the bay that I bought myself a fishing net and a bucket. I literally spent hours fishing every morning. It was not as easy as it looked... I caught lots of tiny little fish and shrimps, but the large fish were cunning and avoided the net."*
George:	"Yes, they see the net as a predator and they can sense it as soon as you put it in the water – so they avoid it."
Cassey:	*"One morning I was fishing happily when I caught sight of a dark shape lurking beneath the clear surface of the water. It was approaching my sister rapidly. She screamed out to my mom and dad, "There's a creature in the water, it's an..." I was nearby on the rocks fishing, but I sprang into action. I waded through the deep water, poised my net and with a quick movement I scooped up the ominous creature. It was huge...so huge that its soft, pink, fleshy tentacles were hanging over the side of the net. Its body was dragging the net down. It started to struggle, using all its strength to try and escape..."*
George:	"Wow. It sounds like something out of a Hollywood movie. You were so brave!"
Cassey:	*"Not really... I was so alarmed that I thrust the net over to my dad. He's scared of things like snakes and he didn't like this creature much. He just dropped it back into the water. In amazement we watched it speed off like a comet, head first, legs behind. It was furious!* *Then we were really disappointed. "Why did you let it go?" we asked.*
George:	"You could have sold it to a restaurant. It would have made a delicious meal! Did you ever find out exactly what it was?"
Cassey:	*"I thought I knew what our mystery catch was, but I looked it up in a reference book anyway and there it was... an octopus!"*
George:	"What an incredible story! I wonder if any of our listeners can beat that..."

Radio Scripts tell *stories* using **DIALOGUE**.

Think about the characters in the radio script. Imagine what it would be like if you met them.

Think about:

- their appearance
- their character
- how they feel

Now imagine the places they've been to. These places could be the setting for a story. Think of a plot for each character and their setting. What events could take place in these places? Develop the plots for these stories. Write the stories.

For example:

- Eric meets a polar bear
- Cassey catches an octopus
- Kegi gets caught in a hurricane
- Jacob's safari bus breaks down
- Agnesa meets Count Dracula
- Noah gets lost in the tropical rainforest
- Madison finds herself lost in the Grand Bazaar

I am:

- eating frogs' legs in France.

- feeling sick because I just ate a creamy, milk pudding in Turkey, but I found out it is made of chicken.

- recovering after eating an extra hot chili for breakfast on the plane, that nearly sent me leaping through the roof.

- eating goat cheese pasta in France, and I don't like it.

- concerned that the menu in the UK includes eel, wood pigeon and squid.

- scared of a wild horse who has poked his head through the window of my car and is eating my picnic in the New Forest in England.

- looking up to the top of Mount Everest in Nepal but it's a long way up.

- eating octopus in Japan which is interesting and then I'm taking a river trip in the dragon boat – cool!

- attending a wedding in India, but it is the rainy season, so we've had to put a cover over the venue.

- running round the Tea Garden in Bangladesh, but an insect has stung me and I'm swelling up.

- sight seeing in Giza in Egypt, looking at the famous pyramids which are tombs of pharaohs who died 4000 years ago.

- watching the Victoria Falls (a waterfall) plunge over the cliff in Zimbabwe and there is a great cloud of spray rising in the air.

- loving the sunset in Marakesh, because the sky is a huge ball of red fire.

- shopping in the street bazaar in Morocco and looking at some handmade carpets laid out in the street for sale.

- walking through the mountains in Poland, but I'm scared I might get eaten by a bear or a wolf.

- sunbathing on a white sandy beach in Australia because it is paradise.

> **Can you add some more? Write about the unusual things you see when you travel.**

Sentences come in all shapes and sizes.

1. This is a **simple sentence**.

   I am eating frogs' legs in France.

2. These sentences are **compound sentences** - joining two simple sentences, using and or but.

   I am eating goat cheese *and* I don't like it.

   I am running around the tea garden *but* I have been stung.

3. Use a conjunction or connective to join ideas in **complex sentences**.

   As I am in Egypt, I'm looking at the famous pyramids.

   I love the sunset in Marakesh *because* the sky is a red ball of fire.

   I am shopping in Turkey, *until* ten o'clock.

4. These sentences use a **subordinate clause**.

   Despite the fact I'm eating pigeon, I am enjoying my dinner in London.

   I was walking through the mountains, *when I saw a bear.*

   On the plane to Turkey, I was enjoying my breakfast until I ate a hot chili.

This sentence has a clause in the middle of it.

   The dragon boat, *that is taking me on a river trip,* is seen in Japan.

- I don't like frogs' legs.

  This is a **statement**.

- How tall is Mount Everest?

  This is a **question**.

- Eat up that squid.

  This is a **command** or an **instruction**.

- That's disgusting!

  This is an **exclamation**.

Time to imagine...
You are going on an expedition to the FROZEN north.

It is very COLD

What clothes would you pack in your backpack?

I would pack warm clothes like:

- a hooded or a fur-lined jacket
- some insulated boots
- a pair of fur-lined gloves
- a warm, fluffy fleece
- a soft wool jacket
- some ski pants

They would have to be:

robust	tear resistant	windproof
rain-proof	weatherproof	wind resistant
warm	fleecy	light weight
comfortable	tough	insulated
hard-wearing	durable	waterproof

To carry my kit I'd need a backpack that:

- is comfortable
- has padded shoulder straps
- has large roomy compartments
- has pockets to fit essentials
- has an emergency kit

> Make some notes.
> **Think about:**

1.
- What was the weather like?
- When did you go?
- Where did you go to?
- Who went on the expedition?
- What transportation did you use?

    (reindeer, cable car, sleigh, Husky, boat, railroad, helicopter, plane)

2.
- How did you camp?
- How did you pitch your tent in the snow?
- Did you light a fire?
- What food did you eat?
- What did you do?
- What did you see?
- Which animals?
- What were they doing?
- Did anything happen?
- Did anything go wrong?

3.
- How did your expedition end?
- How did you feel about it?

Characters: Eric and Uncle Pete

Setting: The frozen north

> **Plan and write a story about your own expedition to the frozen north.**

Interesting opening sentence to grab readers' attention:

Uncle Pete and I tramped through the thick, white snow all day, without seeing anyone, but we were not prepared for what we would meet...

Beginning Paragraph:

- Eric and Uncle Pete walk for days across the snow
- It is cold.
- They don't meet anyone.
- They set up camp in a hut?
    - a tent?
    - an igloo?

Middle Paragraph: Develop the plot
(A discovery triggers some actions that lead to a crisis)

- Uncle Pete prepares a meal of fish that he has caught.
- Eric is digging in the snow, building a cave.
- Suddenly, he feels a hard object in the snow and then another.
- He scrapes around in the snow with his hand.
- He discovers a skeleton with a jaw full of sharp teeth.
- Bones in the snow! He feels horror and fear.

End Paragraph: Resolution

- Uncle Paul has a degree in archaeology.
- He examines the bones.
- He is amazed because it is the skeleton of an amazing prehistoric creature that lived in the neolithic period.
- The next day, they travel in a sleigh pulled by Husky dogs to the nearest town to report their find.
- It is an important discovery.
- They are interviewed on T.V.

You could vary the order of your story by starting right in the action.

I was not prepared for what I saw in front of me. Besides the pile of crystal snow I had just dug out, I saw that I had exposed the skeleton of a jaw full of razor sharp teeth. I dug away the snow a bit more to reveal the skeleton of a head cut into the snow like a diamond. The two dark hollows, where the eyes had been, stared up at me. I viewed the scene with apprehension. Then, I scraped away more snow with my hands and felt the bones of the neck. BONES! A SKELETON! RIGHT IN FRONT OF ME! I was filled with fear and thrill all at the same time. Had I made some amazing discovery?

Let's go out on SAFARI

You read in the newspaper some details about a safari vacation in Africa, but the sentences have gotten mixed up. See if you can write them in the right order. Use 3 paragraphs.

- Book now. It will cost...
- Then you will see herds of zebras and elephants.
- In the evening you will eat dinner
- It will be hot and dry and there will be no rain.
- You will pull up to watch giraffes
- Come on an amazing safari vacation.
- After this, you will ride by Mount Kilimanjaro.
- around a glowing campfire.
- Imagine riding through the African bush.
- At night you will sleep in a tent.
- and monkeys.
- You will ride on a well trained horse at a fast pace
- for six hours a day.

How did you do? Check your answers here:

- Come on an amazing safari vacation.
- It will be hot, dry
- and there will be no rain.
- You will ride a well trained horse
- at a fast pace
- for six hours a day.

- Imagine riding through the African bush.
- You will pull up and watch giraffes
- and monkeys.
- Then you will see herds of zebras and elephants.

- After this, you will ride by Mount Kilimanjaro.
- In the evening you will eat dinner around a glowing camp fire.
- At night you will sleep in a tent.
- Book now. It will cost...

Imagine you went on a safari vacation...

- Where did you go exactly?
- Who went with you?
- What did you take with you?
- What was the weather like?
- What transportation did you use?

- What did you see?
- Which animals?
- What were they doing?
- Did anything exciting happen here?
- Was there danger to people?

- How was the situation resolved?
- How does the story end?

The newspaper article has persuaded you to go on a safari vacation. Write your story.

Characters: me, horse   **Setting:** African bush

Interesting opening sentence, to grab reader's attention:

As I stopped to let my horse drink from the water hole, I became aware that I was not alone... (start with action)

Introduction:

- I heard rustling in the bushes.
- I felt nervous.
- My horse seemed restless as if it sensed danger.
- A lion appeared.

Middle Paragraph:

- The lion was about to attack.
- We galloped at top speed across the savannah.
- The lion was running after us.
- My heart was beating loudly.
- I was terrified.
- The horse was going faster and faster.

End Paragraph:

- We arrived at camp and closed the gate.
- The lion had lost interest and wandered away.
- I told the rangers how I escaped a lion attack.
- I felt very lucky to be alive.

As I stopped to let my horse drink from the waterhole, I became aware that I was not alone. My horse snorted. He was agitated and shook his mane. It was at that moment I spied, out of the corner of my eye, the gold shape of a huge beast, his muscles flexed as he crouched in the shrubs a few feet away. His eyes were fixed on me as he waited to pounce. I commanded my horse,
"Go boy!" We headed off across the plain, in the direction of camp. We were running for our lives. Behind us, I could hear the heavy panting of the creature, who was in hot pursuit. He was on our tail. He was outrunning us...

Continue the story. You could use the following sentence to end:
On that vacation I learned that, although the savannah is beautiful, it is a dangerous place full of predators.

"Today I want you listeners to send in your stories about the most **exciting places you have visited**. Text or email the show now…"

"We have a text from Jacob. He says…"

I traveled on a crowded bus to Nairobi in Kenya and passed giraffes, which were munching leaves from acacia trees… herds of elephants, which were drinking from a water hole and zebras, which were galloping across the plains. There was a flock of bright pink flamingos wading through the lake.

"Oh, I'd love to have been there."

"Agnesa has been back to Romania. She says…"

I walked through a forest and saw a fairy-tale castle where, it is said, a vampire lives - Count Dracula himself. Did you know that Count Dracula was a real prince who lived in Transylvania in the Middle Ages?

"Eeek!"

"Now its Kegi's turn. She takes us on a journey to the Caribbean. To a land where they grow sugar, bananas and coconuts. I'm making myself hungry."

"I stayed with my grandparents in the Caribbean."

"It's gorgeous there, isn't it? Tell us what you saw."

"It's absolutely gorgeous there. It's always hot. There are beaches of white sand, lined with palm trees. I saw the most incredible view of a waterfall across the valley. I dived down into the pink coral reefs. Amazing!

The people are really friendly and they know how to enjoy themselves, especially when they have a carnival. The costumes are so colorful and everyone joins in and dances to the music of the steel drums.

It's not always good to be in the Caribbean. My grandpa told me that some of the islands are built on ancient volcanoes, so the beaches have black sand. He also told me that the worst thing about life in the Caribbean is the hurricanes. They are strong winds that cause terrible damage. If one is coming you may have to barricade yourself in your house or even evacuate until the storm is over."

"Scary stuff, but I would still love to be there."

Let's get *dressed up* and *go out* for the day.

Mrs. Barker, the teacher, asks her class:

- What special events have you been to?
- Where did you go?
- What did you do there?
- Did you enjoy the day?
- Why?

Weddings are *very* **special**. They are a time for the *whole* family to celebrate.

My cousin looked gorgeous as a bride. She had a long white dress trimmed with lace and a long veil with a train, which the bridesmaids carried.

When Uncle Toby married Laura, they made some promises in the church and then they put rings on each others' fingers. As they walked down the aisle, we sprinkled them with rose petals.

I went to a wedding in a big country house. There was a ceremony, followed by a delicious meal called a wedding breakfast and then we danced. The most embarrassing part of the evening was when Dad made his speech – or on second thought – maybe it was my mom's dancing.

My brother's wedding photos were taken on the terrace of the venue in the Seychelles as the sun set and turned into a big ball of fire.

My older brother married his bride in Turkey so we had to take our special outfits on a long flight. My mom had a big hatbox in her carry-on luggage, which she didn't want to get squashed. I carried two wedding bears, dressed as a bride and groom, on my lap.

On the day of my cousin's wedding, we put on our clothes in the hotel and then we took a taxi to the church. The taxi driver got lost. He didn't know where the church was. Panic! We didn't want to miss the wedding. Fortunately, we still arrived before the bride.

My auntie looked gorgeous. She wore a stunning red sari for her wedding day. She wore lots of gold jewelry and her hands and feet were painted in beautiful patterns with henna. The bride and groom wore huge garlands of fresh flowers.

When my second cousin got married, the bride arrived with a veil to cover her face. They both took steps towards the fire to make their promises, before they were joined together with a long sash and then petals were thrown all over them.

What other **special events** have *you* been to?

Harry writes:

It was very special when I went to the State Capitol Building to see my uncle become the governor. We watched the swearing-in ceremony from special seating in the building.

At the start of the ceremony, my uncle came into the room with some other people. He was dressed in his best suit with a red tie. The first thing he did was walk to the podium in the center of the room. Then, everyone stood up for the Pledge of Allegiance.

The man read out some vows to the state and country. After this, he handed over the seal of the state to my uncle, so now he can do all the things that a governor can do. My uncle then promised to serve the state. He bowed and everyone shouted. Some people were crying because they were so happy. I felt very proud of my uncle. I felt honored to have been invited because it was a once in a lifetime opportunity.

Every July 4th is special because we celebrate the signing of the Declaration of Independence. People meet in the town center and they have picnics and barbecues.
Then we watch the fireworks. It's amazing!

Every **NATION** has SPECIAL DAYS & RELIGIOUS FESTIVALS.

For example:

New Year, Independence Day, Bastille Day in France, Christmas, Easter, Thanksgiving, Hanukkah, Holi, Ramadan, Eid, Diwali, Buddha Jayanti Festival, Vaisakhi, or maybe Mother's Day or Father's Day or Mardi Gras (Shrove Tuesday).

How do you celebrate?

What do you eat?

What do you wear?

How long does the celebration go on?

Describe special features of your day.

Now, it's your turn to write about a special event.

Recount a personal experience:

Write the events in the **order they happened**. Make your writing interesting. **Join ideas with connectives**. Then you can make some **personal comments**.

- who
- where
- what
- why
- when

it happened to you

Let's party. What *birthday parties* have *you* been to recently?

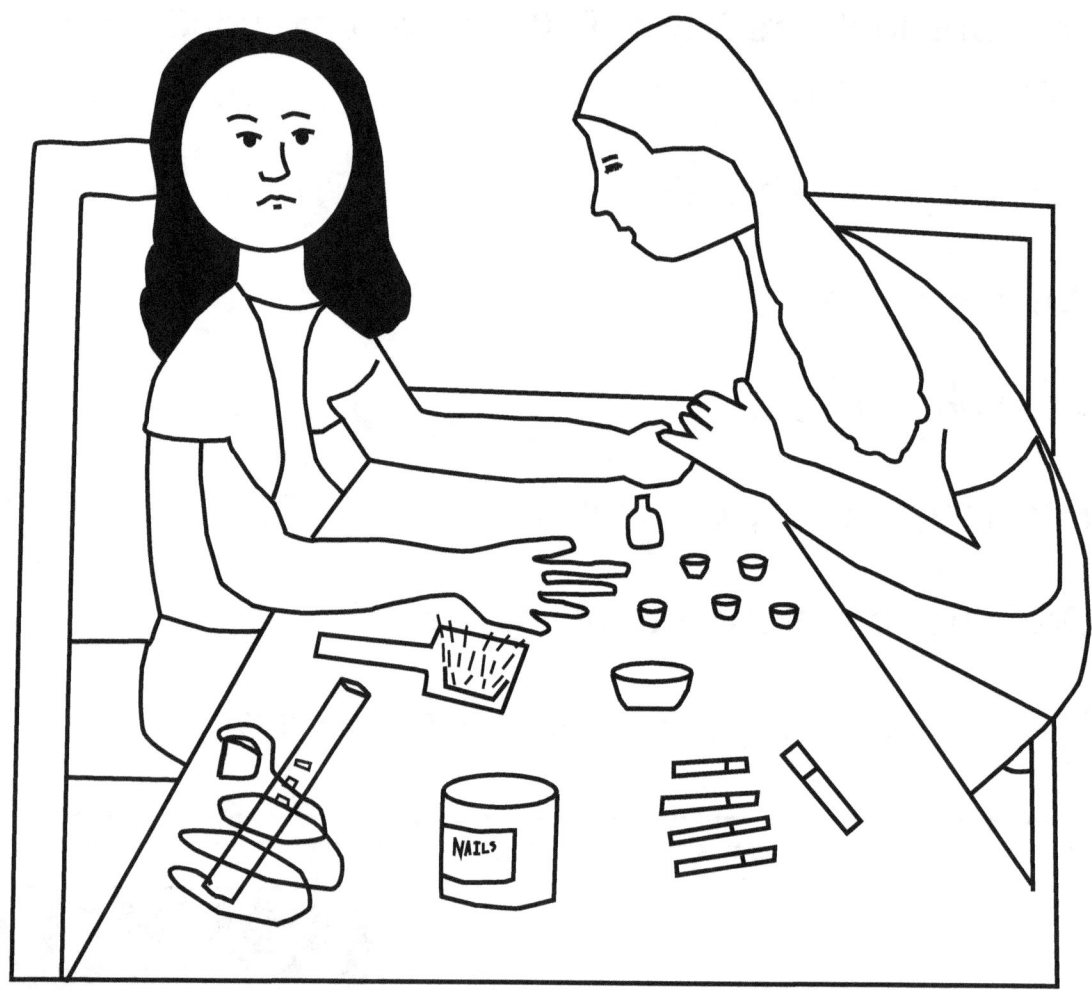

"I had a marvelous makeover party," says Sophie.
This really cool lady called Leyla came to my house with her daughter Roxie. They put a big plastic cloth on the table and laid out tons of natural beauty products in rows: lipsticks, glosses, glittery eye shadows and mascaras that you spray on your lashes to make them bright and colorful. When my friends arrived, they couldn't make up their minds which colors to choose because there was so much choice.

 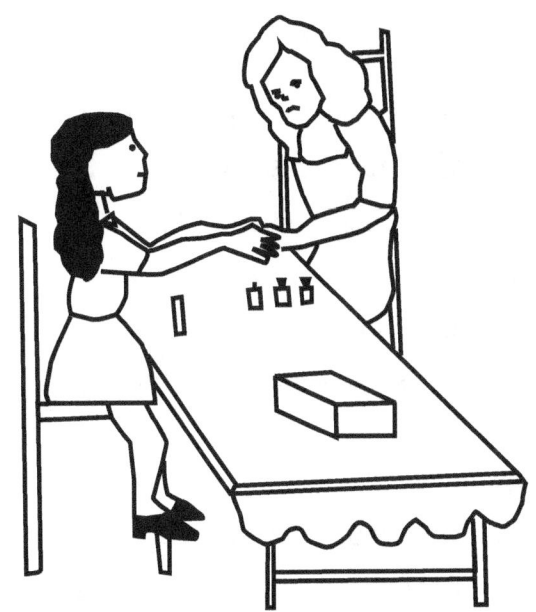

Later Leyla and Roxie helped us style our hair. Some children had lots of curls put in with the curling iron, but others straightened their hair and sprayed it with glitter spray. Next, Leyla painted our nails in dazzling fluorescent colors and she added spots and glittery flowers. She even put a fake diamond on my big toe. After this, Roxie applied our favorite make-up and I wore the same lip gloss as the star on my favorite TV show.

Finally, my brother and his friend Karl had their faces painted. Leyla said that they could be pirates... or vampires... or even ghosts... but they chose to be pop stars. They looked terrific.

When the dancing started the boys showed off, because they did all these crazy dance routines they had learned during vacation last summer.

When my mom saw my make-up, at the end of the party, she went, "Wow! You look great!" but all Dad said was,
"Hope it will wash off before school on Monday."

What did you like about the party?
I liked:
The fruity lip glosses because they tasted so good.
My bright pink nails because they were so pretty.
The glittery eye shadow because it is worn by celebrities.
My curly hair because I looked different.
The diamonds on my toes which made me look like a pop star.
The make-up comes in colorful boxes, which I could buy as presents for my friends.

I won't forget my 9th birthday party on the 4th of August, at the community center. I invited my whole class, from 3-6pm.

Why won't I forget it?

Marvelous Matt came to entertain us and he brought the cutest creatures to help him. Carrie his cockatoo helped do card tricks using her beak.

Matt juggled with balls. He balanced on a unicycle with a closed container on his head. Guess what was inside? It was a furry tarantula called Susie. We screamed.

After this, he dressed up a boy called Louis in a scarecrow costume with a funny wig. Then, he said the scarecrow had a special friend and he made him hold Samuel, a rat. Louis hated the feel of the rat's tail in his hand and started making funny faces, so we all howled with laughter.

Next, Matt told us to close our eyes and count to ten. This trick, he said, involved real danger. When we opened our eyes, Matt had an anaconda, a big patterned snake, around his neck like a scarf.

What was my favorite part of the party?

At the end of the party, Matt said we could meet the animals. Out of his top hat, he produced three gorgeous ferrets with soft fur. We were allowed to handle all the gorgeous pets, while Matt gave us lots of information about them. It was my best party ever.

How did *you* **celebrate** your birthday?

Look! Here are some SIMPLE sentences.

- I had a gym party. It was exhausting.
- I had a magician. He pulled a rabbit out of his hat.
- I had a bouncy castle. I felt sick.
- We had a boat trip on the river. It lasted for one hour.
- I went in a go-kart. It was exciting.

Look! COMPOUND sentences join two ideas with BUT or AND.

- I celebrated my birthday with a soccer game and we had a picnic with hot dogs, hamburgers and fries.
- I had a barbecue in my backyard but Dad burned the hot dogs.
- We went on a trip to the movies and we saw the latest film. (Can you guess which one?)
- I had a bowling party but my team lost.
- I had a swimming party and we went down the slide twenty-five times. (What fun!)
- We went to a dance club and I won a prize for being the best dancer.
- It was interesting at the railroad museum but my friend got in trouble. (He shouldn't have touched that machine!)

WOW! Here are some COMPLEX SENTENCES. You can use a CONNECTIVE.

- I won the prize at the dance party because I had the best costume.
- You can bounce all evening if you go to a trampoline party.
- You can shoot people with paint guns when you go to a paintball party.
- We played a game spotting places while we were on the helicopter ride.

You can use a COMMA after a sub clause.

- On a tour around the baseball stadium, we were shown the lockers of famous players.
- As I climbed the rock face, I felt excited.
- Despite having an instructor, I found it terrifying to rappel from the top of the cliff.

You can TURN SENTENCES AROUND to make them interesting.

- Before we saw the Broadway show at the theater, we had burgers and fries.
- We had burgers and fries, before we saw the Broadway show.
- At the drama workshop, the lady instructed,
  "When I say ice cream, everyone must smile and run around as if you are really happy - but when I say no ice cream, you must stop still, like a statue and look really sad." (direct speech)
  At the drama workshop, the lady said that we were to say ice cream and run around as if we were really happy. (reported speech)

Use a VARIETY OF SENTENCES to make your writing interesting.
Now, write some more of your own.

Write an invitation to your party or plan a party for your brother, sister, niece, nephew or a neighbor.

Dear ....

Please come to my themed party

which is a ....

It is on .... at ....

between .... and ....

You will need to wear a costume, which must consist of ....

You will take part in lots of activities, including ....

Hope you can come.

Love

....

Please R.S.V.P.

I will be pleased to come to your .... theme party.

Love from,

....

Themed Parties

Can be at:
- home
- in a hall
- in a church hall
- in a tent
- in the backyard
- in the park

You can have:
- games
- music
- dancing
- make over
- a popcorn machine

You can go:
- kayaking
- bowling
- swimming
- laser tag
- to a theme park
- to the movies
- on a boat trip
- on a helicopter ride
- practice archery
- go-karting
- ride an all-terrain vehicle
- do water sports
- to the zoo

It can be a:
- princess party
- bowling party
- pirate party
- craft party
- spaceman party
- backwards party
- diva party
- desert island party
- alien party
- costume party
- football party

You can do:
- experiments at the science party.
- make things at the craft party.
- slide down the slide at the swimming party.
- eat delicious pizza at the restaurant.
- see the latest film at the movies.
- go to a Broadway musical at a New York theater.
- play games at a bowling party.
- throw paint at your friends at a paintball party.
- spot things on the ground at a hot air ballooning party.

What we eat

Savory foods like:
- sandwiches
- hot dogs
- burgers and fries
- pizza
- chips

Sweet foods like:
- chocolate cake
- ice cream
- birthday cake
- **soda**

What I thought of the party

It was:

pleasing	amusing	dreary
exciting	humorous	tiresome
delightful	entertaining	unexciting
happy	boring	monotonous
fun	dull	uninteresting
hilarious	tedious	thrilling

Use these questions to help you plan some writing about your party or one held by a friend.

- When was the party? (It was on... at...)
- Where was the party?
- Who was there?
- What did you eat?
- What did you wear?

- What did you do/play?
- Did anything exciting happen?
- Did anything go wrong?
- Was there a problem or complication?
- Did some tension build up? For example, Lucy ate too much and felt sick.

- How was this resolved?
- How did the party end?
- Did you get a prize, a party bag or a balloon?
- What did you think of it?

If you are writing a diary entry, write details about what you did:

1. What did you make at the craft party?

2. Did you make jewelry, clothes, flowers, a tie-dyed scarf or something else?

3. What did you need? (tissue paper, scissors, glue)

4. Write the steps you did to make them.

5. What was it like when you finished it?

- In the same way, THINK ....
- What experiments did you do at the science party?
- What activities did you do at the gym?
- What was the film like you saw at the movies?

Use the questions to write about any party you've been to.

Now write a story or diary entry about a party.

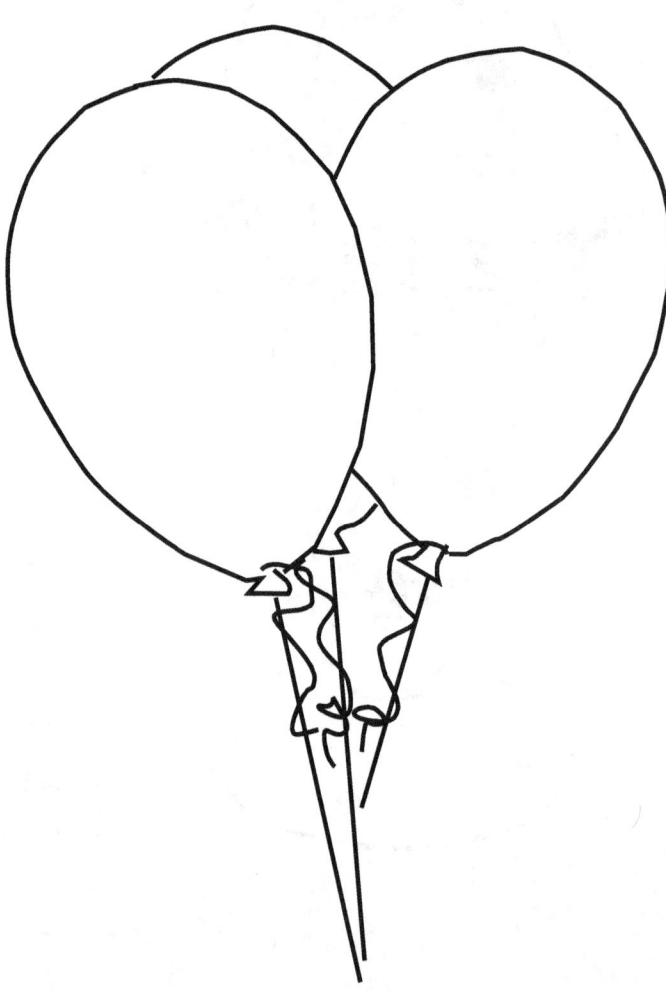

Make a poster

Come to 'Tooty Fruity' **kids' club** for your **special celebration,** for boys and girls aged ....

- **Enjoy** our **tasty fruit juices** at the juice bar, like ....
- **Chill out** with your friends in our games room.
- **Watch** ....
- **Play on** ....
- **Listen to** ....
- **Dance** to our **karaoke machine**, from **6-9pm,** to the sound of .... your **fave band**.

Let's <u>RELAX</u>.
Let's <u>not</u> go far.

Mrs. Barker gets her class to write about what they like to do during the weekend. She mounts the work on the wall.

Twins, Gareth and Gemma, write about a summer barbecue.

It was July and Mom was away for the weekend. It was baking hot in our backyard and we were sizzling up. Dad had summoned up enough energy to fill the kiddie pool. I'd been running across the garden and leaping in, splashing everyone. Then Dad said,

"Enough of that. Get your shoes on. We're going to have a barbecue and need to get to (the supermarket) 'Fresco' before it closes, to get the food."

Soon, we were pushing the rattly old cart down the meat aisle, where Dad carefully selected some lamb that was chopped into cubes. (Dad's a great cook and he seemed to know what he was doing.) Next stop was the fruit and vegetable counter.
"Put in some red onions, juicy tomatoes and some fresh mint leaves," he ordered, "then, get a cucumber and a pack of those green leaves...." At that point his voice trailed off because he had seen an old friend he used to work with.
"Get the rest of the items on the list, Gareth, while I have a quick word with Cody," he boomed, thrusting the list into my hands. That's when I zoomed up and down the aisles with my cart, trying to decipher (understand) some strange words on the list – red wine vinegar, paprika – and ... a box of ground cumin which was up high. I stood on tiptoes to reach it, but it was too high ... I accidentally set off an avalanche of boxes. They fell one by one slowly off the shelf and hit the floor with a bang!

"I'm really sorry," I stammered to the angry assistant. Dad was still chatting away so he wasn't going to help me clean up the mess. Some of the boxes had opened and spilled out.
"I'll call for a cleaner," snapped the Fresco assistant. At that point I was gone like a shot. I was heading for the check out – though I threw in a few extras on the way: a pack of freshly baked cookies from the in-store bakery, extra value chips and a huge chocolate cake on special offer.
"Can't be bad," I said to myself. As Dad joined me, panting and red faced, he started to scan the items through the automatic check out. There was a problem. The cucumber wouldn't scan and I noticed that the same assistant was coming over. She was still furious so I sidled off to wait by the door. As I saw Dad type his PIN into the machine to pay, I observed that he had not even noticed my additions to the cart.

Gemma writes:

When the sun comes out you have to make the most of it. It was Sunday and it was boiling hot. Mom was away at a business conference, so Dad decided to do a barbecue.

Dad liked to cook food on the blazing hot coals with his tongs because he pretended he was a TV Master chef. The night before the barbecue he covered the meat in spicy stuff – paprika, cumin and olive oil and he put it in the fridge overnight to marinate to give the meat flavor. At two o'clock, he lit the barbecue, donned his apron and put cubes of meat on skewers. Then he put them on the grill and turned them over until they were brown. It was my job to help Dad in the kitchen, to mix onions, tomatoes and spices together in a bowl to make a sauce. I tasted a small spoonful

"Wow! It's very tangy. Perhaps a little too much spice," I said to myself, but there was no time to start again so I took it outside and put it on the table.

Soon I heard a bang on the door and I ran to answer it. On the stoop, I saw Cody and his new girl friend who had been given a last minute invitation by Dad. They smiled at me and they thrust a box of chocolates into my hand. I took them through to the yard and everyone stood around chatting. It was not long before we lined up with our plates for a kebab, a dollop of sauce and some green salad.

"Mmm this salsa is good," said Cody's girlfriend, smiling. "Did you make it? Delicious!" At that moment Grandad took a big mouthful of food...but the hot spice made him choke violently and he dropped his plate of food on the grass. In an instant, the dog dived on it and wolfed it down, but it was hot. His tongue was on fire. He leaped around like a crazy creature. He knocked the barbecue and it tipped...

"HELP!" shouted Dad. "It's going O V E R..."

For a moment, chaos reigned in the back garden of 4 Holly Road. In a T.V. sketch it would have been hilarious... but at that moment nobody was smiling because the yard was on fire. Dad and Cody were frantically trying to beat out the flames. There were kebabs everywhere on the grass. Grandad, who was holding his cell phone, looked puzzled as he wondered whether to call the fire department. In an effort to restore order I headed to the kitchen, followed by Cody's girlfriend, and we found a gooey chocolate cake for dessert. I was surprised because Dad usually chose healthy things like yogurt or fruit. We cut the cake into slices, took it outside and laid it on the table. To our relief the fire was out, but at that moment, to add to the chaos, my horrid brother, Gareth, raced across the garden with the dog and jumped into the kiddie pool with a huge splash. Everything was soaked. Just then Mom phoned to see how we were doing. "We're having an amazing time," I replied. "Amazing!"

How did Gareth plan his story?

Look at the beginning sentences of the story. Each one starts with a <u>different</u> word.

It was a July day and...

The weather was...

Dad had...

but Gareth...

Then Dad decided to have a...

so he said, "Get ready..."

....

Soon they were...

Dad selected some...

and then he went to...

At that point he met...

He said to Gareth, "Get..."

Gareth zoomed up the supermarket aisle to get...

He stood on... but it was too...

Then he caused... and...

....

He said, "..." to the...

The angry woman called a...

Gareth headed for... but...

When Dad joined him, there was...

so he... but...

Gareth hid by... so...

Use the plan to write this story.

Introduction   Make a plan:

- The characters are...
- The setting is...
- The plot is...

Paragraph 1

- hot day
- kiddie pool out
- sitting in yard
- decide to have a barbecue
- go to the supermarket to buy the food

....

What happens next? Is there a problem? Is there tension?

Paragraph 2

- Gareth pushes the cart
- collects up ingredients for barbecue - lamb, onions, salad
- Dad sees friend and goes over to talk to him
- Gareth left to get rest of items
- shelf too high
- reaches up, but knocks down boxes with a bang

....

How is the situation resolved?

Paragraph 3

- says he is sorry to store assistant
- she gets cleaner
- Gareth heads for checkout
- puts extra items in cart
- Dad joins him and doesn't notice the extra items
- problem at register so same angry assistant comes over
- Gareth waits for Dad by door

How did Gemma plan her story?

Look at the beginning sentences of the story. Each one starts with a <u>different</u> word.

When the sun comes out...

It was Sunday and it was...

Dad decided to have a... because...

He pretended he was a master chef on T.V. so he...

At two o' clock, Dad lit the barbecue. He... and...

....

I hear a... so...

On the stoop are... who...

They thrust... and we...

Everyone stood around...

It was not long before...

Grandad took a mouthful but...

When he choked, he dropped...

The dog dived... and... but...

He knocked... Dad shouted...

....

Chaos reigned at...

No one was smiling because the garden was...

Dad and Cody were trying to...

I headed to the kitchen to get... followed by....

Then my brother... and jumped...

When my mom phoned...

Introduction   Make a plan:

- The characters are...
- The setting is...
- The plot is...

Paragraph 1

- boiling hot day
- family plan barbecue - special recipe
- Dad puts meat in fridge overnight

....

Paragraph 2

- afternoon 2:30 pm
- Dad is cooking the meat
- Gemma helps mix the saue
- Cody and his new girlfriend arrive
- We eat
- Cody's girlfriend comments that the food is good
- Grandad chokes - drops plate
- dog knocks over barbecue
- Dad screams for help

....

Paragraph 3

- try to put out shrub on fire
- beat out flames
- Grandad is going to call fire department
- get out dessert
- brother jumps kiddie pool with a splash
- Mom phones

> Now it's your turn to write the story.

Priya, Joshua, Nina, Sandy, Rebecca and Arthur spend Saturday at the park. They describe what they saw.

I went down to the park and...

Priya writes...

On Saturday we put a cozy sheet on the grass under the <u>shady</u> tree and had a <u>delicious</u> picnic. We <u>lazed</u> about all afternoon.

Nina says...

When I went down to the **sparkling** lake with Mom, we sat on the bench looking at the reflection of green trees that **shimmered** in the water. It looked lovely.

Tom and I leaned our bike up against the tree and sat on a bench by the lake. There, we stared down into the green water and witnessed thousands of newly hatched tadpoles swimming in the <u>shallow</u> water. I wanted to go home and get a bucket, but Tom wanted to get an ice cream at the café.

Describe and use words to create word pictures. You will help your reader conjure up the atmosphere. Choose the right word.

Sandy says...

We walked around the cool lake and leaned over the bridge to watch a crane paddle by. He had a white masked face. On the beach, two proud Goldeneye ducks **preened** their feathers, **flapped** their wings and **glided** across the lake, forming little ripples on the water. Two mallards rested by the water's edge until a dog **bounded** up on to the beach barking...and **splashed** about in the cool water. When he barked they swam off into the distance.

Arthur says...

I sat on a bench and watched the dogs with their owners. There were so many different breeds of dog, including spotty Dalmations, cute Cocker Spaniels with long floppy ears and sweet Jack Russels. The owners threw balls for their dogs to fetch and they bounded off across the park with their tails wagging. A small terrier padded up to me for a stroke.

> I went fishing by the lake. The water was <u>crystal clear</u>; some gnats danced above the water. I didn't catch anything.

Priya writes...

The grass was <u>dotted</u> with little groups of people, chatting, sunbathing and picnicking, but my family – that's Grandma, Mom and my three aunts and all my cousins – got into teams and played a big game of baseball. You should have seen Auntie Parminder run. As for me I scored the highest number of runs.

Joshua writes...

I went to the park and lay on the grass and closed my eyes. It was so **<u>tranquil</u>**, so <u>peaceful</u> and so <u>quiet</u>. All I could hear was the <u>rhythmic</u> sound of balls hitting the tennis rackets as people played tennis in the park. It was like <u>music to my ears</u>.

I helped Auntie Kieran push her **<u>cute</u>** baby around the park. We stopped by the lake to take a picture of baby in her sunbonnet, against the background of **<u>pretty</u>** trees by the lake. We said 'smile.' She **<u>beamed</u>** at us and we captured her smile.

Rebecca writes...

I listened to the noise of the fair. The fairground man <u>**yelled**</u>, "Shall I make the ride go faster and even faster!" Soon his voice was drowned out by the screaming riders <u>**whizzing**</u> around.

I went to a wonderful fair at the park. I saw hundreds of people **mingling** together. They were **munching** on cotton candy, doughnuts and popcorn. They were playing games and going on rides.

The fairground men shouted: "Roll Up Roll Up! Come and win a football on the 'prize every time stall.' It's only 99 cents a turn."

"**Shoot** down the cans and win a prize."

"**Smash** down the china and win a prize."

"**Ride** 'Pirate Pete's' big dipper."

"**Come** on tiny tots, ride the land train."

"**Whizz** around on the teacup ride."

"What should we go on first - the ghost train... the hall of mirrors?" It was hard to decide.

I saw a small child who had wandered away from his mom. His tears were dripping down his cheeks, but a _kind_ policeman on duty ran over to hep him and the child was soon reunited with his mom.

What did you see when you went to the park?

(on the grass, at the fair, in the tennis courts, by the lake)

- Who was there?
- What did they wear?
- Why are they there?
- What are the people doing?
- What wildlife did you see?
- Did anything interesting happen?

Use the questions to help you write your own description of an afternoon in the park.

Let's <u>GO OUT</u>

Think of an outing you have enjoyed. It may have been an outing with your family, with your school, or an after-school club.

Answer these questions in sentences. Start each sentence with a new word.

- Where did you go?
- When did you go?
- What time did you leave?
- Who went with you?
- How did you get there?

- What did you do?
- What interesting things happened on the outing?

- Did you go to the fair or carnival?
- Which rides did you go on?
- What did you hear, see, feel, taste, smell?
- How did you feel? *(excited, happy, scared)*
- What did you win?
- What did you buy?

- How did you feel as you went home?
- What did you enjoy?

Here are some personal responses to help you:

I felt that	I was interested in...	I thought...
I was surprised by...	I found...	I liked the part when...
It was humorous...	It was exciting...	It was funny...

LET'S BRAINSTORM THE FAIR

Add to this list of adjectives and nouns to describe the fair:

fast rides	colorful stalls	amazing prizes
big balloons	bright orange goldfish	delicious cotton candy
scrumptious sweets	mouth watering hot dogs	

Pair up the verbs and adverbs to describe the fair - (screaming loudly.)

yelling	screaming	wailing	shrieking
screaming	shouting	noisily	raucously
boisterously	rowdily	loudly	nervously
fearfully	ecstatically		

throwing	aiming	hurling	tossing
flinging	shooting	skillfully	quickly
cleverly	competently	expertly	

winning	singing	dancing	waving
happily	joyfully	excitedly	eagerly

towering	steeply	soaring	high
whirling	daringly		(add 'ly' or 'ily' to form some adverbs)

Let's go to the beach
Vlad describes his day at the beach

"On the first morning of my vacation, I woke up in my hotel room. The sunlight pierced through the thick green curtains and filled my room with bright light. I grabbed my towel, sunscreen and swimsuit and headed towards the beach. I ran down the steep steps and arrived on the soft sand. I dropped my bag under one of the umbrellas and splashed my pale skin with a handful of sunscreen.

I plunged into the turquoise waves like an arrow, making a foaming splash. I swam deeper and deeper in the cool water, gazing at the beautiful fish that were swimming around the shore. The beach was very busy now. I could hear the sound of waves rolling gently onto the shore, but loud music boomed in the background. The sky was clear blue, with a juicy sun smiling over the beach. Multicolored kites soared proudly, showing off their unique shapes and colors. Bright patterned umbrellas were dug into the ground with bronze-colored people relaxing underneath. The kids were running around laughing and throwing a frisbee, while the teenagers played a game of volleyball, shaking their heads to the beat of the radio. Adults were teaching their youngsters to swim.

Soon the delicious smell of barbecue drifted up to my nose. I emerged from the water with a splish, splosh and clambered up the beach to get some food. The grains of sand stuck on my feet, as if little gems were glued to my toes. As I turned around I could see footprints stamped into the golden sand. I purchased a cardboard carton of fries decorated with little diamonds of salt and a hot dog sizzled to perfection and smothered with mustard and ketchup.

I ate my mouth watering lunch under my umbrella and waited for my body to dry off. After lying in the sun on my beach towel, I got up and began making sandcastles with my bucket and shovel. By the time I finished, it was an impressive fort decorated with seaweed and small shells.

It was now late in the afternoon, so I grabbed my snorkeling gear and went onto the diving platform. It was moving up and down as I went further out. The water beneath got deeper and deeper. I put on my diving gear and I jumped into the water and started to frog leg down. I was surrounded by a coral reef; it was like being in a dream. There were many brightly colored fish and beautiful plants – red, pink, white, green. I dived further down to inspect the coral closer and saw small starfish sunbathing on the reef and shy shell fish poking their heads out of plants, but I was losing breath so I had to go back up.

Back on the beach, the sun was setting and people were leaving. Alone with the sea, I watched the sky turn a tropical orange color with shades of pink and purple. I stared in awe and wonder. The water darkened and the seagulls flew away in the distance. Crabs scurried along the shore and hopped into the sea. I could not wait to come back tomorrow. It was as if the beach had become a part of me."

Can **YOU** find...

Similes – that compare people, things and ideas using like or as

"like an arrow"   *"as if gems were glued to my toes"*

Metaphors – that describe something as being something else

"diamonds of salt"

Onomatopoeia - words which sound like the word they are describing

"I emerged from the water with a splish, splosh"

Alliteration – is the repetition of a consonant sound

"soft sand..."   *"splashed my skin with sunscreen..."*

Personification – giving human qualities to an object

"juicy sun, smiling down on the beach..."
"multicolored kites soared proudly..."

Use **your senses** – What do you hear, see, smell, touch, taste?

"loud music boomed..."   *"smell of barbecue drifted up..."*

Use **good nouns** and **adjectives**.

"turquoise waves"   *"clear blue sky"*
"thick green curtain"

Use **powerful verbs.**

"plunged"   *"grabbed"*   *"pierced"*   *"sizzled"*

Use **verbs** and **adverbs**.

"rolling gently"   **Can you find any more?**

What can you do on a simply *sizzling* <u>**hot**</u> summer day?

You can:

Visit the green park.	Go to the golden beach.
Sit under a shady tree.	Lay on a patterned towel on the yellow sand.
Walk the naughty dog.	Cover yourself in sunscreen.
Munch on a delicious picnic.	Enjoy a cool ice cream.
Play a great game of baseball.	Suck luscious lollipops.
Relax on the new swings.	Play beach ball and frisbee.
Clamber on the play equipment.	Swim in the salty sea.
Hang upside down and climb on the monkey bars.	Paddle your hot feet.
Zoom down the slide.	Collect shiny shells.
Walk through the rose garden.	Construct sand sculptures.

Look for doing words, verbs (stroll, munch).
Look for adjectives and nouns (luscious lollipops, salty sea).
Can you add some more?

Do **you** like <u>eating out of doors</u>?

Make a chart like this one and fill it in.

	PICNIC	**BARBECUE**
Where?	riverbank, park, sandy beach	yard
What was the weather like?	not sunny	simply sizzling
Who went with you?	grandma, family, friends from school, church or club.	auntie, uncle
My favorite food is:	sandwiches, hot dogs, chips	spicy burgers and sweet corn
Food I don't like:		kebabs with spicy salsa
Other things we do:	Play baseball together, feed the ducks on the lake.	
What people say:		"This salsa is delicious. Did you make it?"
What I like about eating outdoors:		

Make a list of summer foods:
- crispy lettuce
- spicy chicken wings
- hot dogs

Help to make a **cool drink** for summer days:

Put the recipe for Pineapple Smoothie in order.

- Put yogurt and fruit into a blender.
- You need yogurt and pineapple.
- Make a pineapple smoothie.
- Take the rind off the pineapple.
- Chop fruit into cubes.
- Drink the smoothie.
- Get an adult to blend the ingredients for 30 seconds.

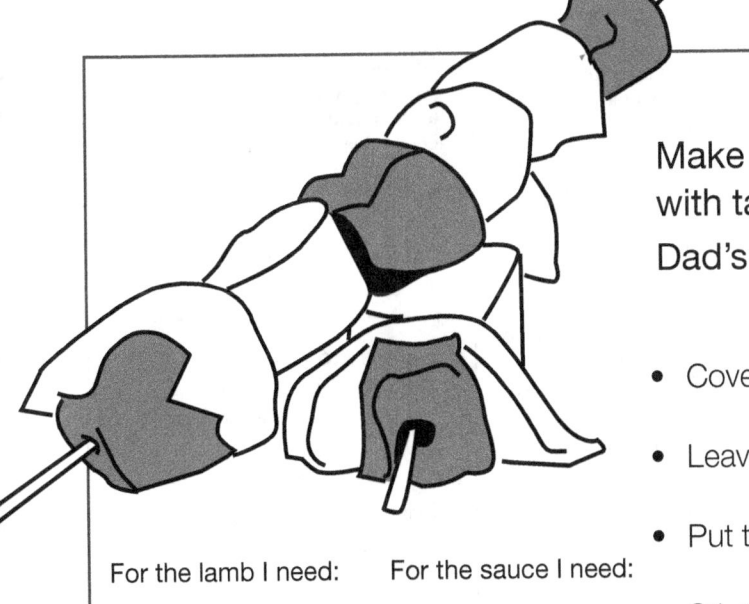

Make a recipe for lamb kebabs with tangy salsa. Use Dad's recipe in Gemma's story.

- Cover the .... in ....
- Leave the .... overnight
- Put the cubes of meat on ....
- Stir the .... in a bowl with ....
- Add .... Pour it ....

For the lamb I need:
- ....
- ....
- ....

For the sauce I need:
- ....
- ....
- ....

Try writing your own recipe for hot dogs or banana smoothie.

Rushford Gazette does a local news feature.

Rushford Gazette Friday June 6th 2029

What's happening in your local area

If you are running an event this week, during the lazy carefree days of summer, place your advertisement here free of charge.

June 11th - 15th Saint Teresa's Elementary School on Holly Road presents 'The Wizard of Oz.' Tickets $5, half price for children. A fun, family musical show. Sure to make you laugh.

July 5th Sponsored race around Rushford Park, to raise money for the Life Boat Association. Collect your sponsor form from Rushford Library.

July 14th - 19th Annual Rushford Cat Show. Come and watch Rushford's posh pets fight it out for the prestigious title 'Cat Of The Year.' Entry free. Please note: entry to this show is only available to Cat Club Members.

July 20th - 27th Are you over 60? Join us on our annual trip to lovely Venice. Take a relaxing gondola ride through the ancient city's maze of narrow waterways. Watch the world go by from the chic cafes around the square. Call our booking line for more information on (847) 555-0215.

The annual Rushford COUNTY SHOW

August 20th - 25th

An event certainly not to be missed. A great family day out.

There are so many animals to see from rabbits and chickens to bulls, cows, sheep, goats, heavy horses and donkeys. There is also a Dog Show, which is free to the public.

Entertainment everyday in the Grand Parade Ground – including brass band, parachute jumping and horse jumping.

A FANTASTIC DAY OUT FOR ALL THE FAMILY. Show opened at 10am by the Mayor of Rushford.

Has RUSHFORD got **TALENT**?

Auditions to take place July 31st from 9am at Rushford Stadium. Showcase your talent in front of a panel of top judges – whether you are good at singing, dancing, acting, impressions or ? We would love to see you there. Huge cash prize for winning act!

July 29th Moms get fit for your summer vacation, while your kids are at day camp. Daily jogging club meets at 9am at the entrance to Rushford Sports Center, followed by coffee and cakes at Mo's Café.

August 8th Come and have a fun day at Rushford Junior High School Fair. Guess the name of our school teddy bear and take part in a costume competition. Open to all ages. Treat yourself to one of our delicious ice creams. All proceeds will go to school's funds to provide P.E. equipment.

August 10th Come and see 'Glitzy Mitzy,' one of the most exciting rock bands of this year, playing live at the Rushford Stadium. To book tickets for this event of the year, call the Rushford Stadium box office or book online at www.rushfordstadiumonline.com. Tickets are nearly sold out.

August 12th Come to St Mary's annual church fair. There will be hundreds of stalls selling local crafts: like handmade soaps, lavender cushions, stunning jewelry, soft toys and handmade clothes. You can also visit our tents selling delicious cakes, pastries, preserves and juicy strawberries that have been grown locally. Visit our flower show and see the incredible displays of colorful blooms. There'll be lots of games for the kids, like 'Splat the Rat,' 'Prize Every time,' 'Lucky Dip' and guess the number of candies in the jar. All proceeds to go to local church funds.

KIDS PLAY

We still have limited places in our vacation package throughout August.

Week 1
Join us for our paintball extravaganza.

Week 2
water sport week – wake boarding, windsurfing, canoeing and white water rafting - sure to be great fun.

Week 3
Extreme sport week – rock climbing, rappeling, bungee jumping and parachute jumping in our super safe center. Fantastic fun.

Week 4
Arts and craft week – your chance to paint a mural in the shopping center, learn filmmaking with a director from Disney.

Public Notices

Save up to 10% when you place an announcement in the Rushford Gazette.

By taking advantage of our online booking system, you can save 10% off the cost of your advertisement.

HAVE FUN! Make a newspaper page and write some advertisements of your own.

Now find the answers to these questions.

- If you are over sixty, what place could you go to?

- If you pay for a 'Kids Play' vacation package, on weeks two and four, what fun activities will you do?

- Where can you go to enter your dog for a competition?

- Holly wants to take her Grandma to her school show. What school does she go to and when is it happening?

- Mrs. Smith has grown some beautiful roses. Where can she show them?

- Where can Mom exercise while the kids are at day camp?

- Some people want to raise money to buy a new lifeboat. What do they have to do?

- Tom is so good at street dancing that he thinks he can win a talent competition. Where can he go?

- Sam's dad is a huge fan of Glitzy Mitzy. Where could he book tickets for her next gig?

- Cleo is a top cat. What does he have to join to win the title 'Cat of the Year'?

- Harry is dressing up as Harry Potter. What school does he go to?

Make up some more questions and see if a friend can answer them.

Imagine you are organizing a *big show* in your town this summer.

Jot some notes down

- Shall we call our show a fair, a festival, or even a carnival?
- Where is the best site?
- Is it a field, a park, a school playground, or somewhere else?
- When should we hold our fair?
- What date should we choose?
- What time will it start or finish?
- What kind of people do we want to come to the show?
- What is the purpose of the show?

Should we have:

- horse rides
- a dog or cat show
- a police demonstration
- a fire engine that children can climb aboard
- competition like costumes

Can you think of some more?

Can you think of some exciting events that will thrill the spectators in the grand ring, like bike riders, parachute teams or a horse jumping competition? Can you write a list?

Things to do

1. Now, make a poster. Write an ad to persuade people to come to your show. Make a program of events like the one on the next page.

2. Write letters asking people to donate items for the fair.

3. Make up some competitions that people can enter. For example, the biggest vegetable competition, best dog, rabbit, cow, pig, horse competition, best painting competition, best cake competition, best flower arrangement. Can you think of anymore?

Rushford village Fair

Saturday July 17th

At: ....

Times: ....

Come and See: ....
....
....
....

Enter our competitions WIN a fabulous prize

- Best flower arrangement, judged 2pm
- Painting competition, judged 2:30pm
- Largest tomato competition, judged 3:30pm
- Cutest pet competition, judged 3:30pm
- Best costume competition, judged 4:00pm

★★★★★★★★★★★★★★★★★★★★★

Entertainment in the GRAND RING starts from 1:30pm.

1:30pm	Grand opening of the fair by the Mayor
	Rushford Cheerleading squad
2:00pm	Wild Bird Display
2:30pm	Rushford Dancers
3:00pm	Sheepdog herding demonstration
3:30pm	Horse jumping competition
4:00pm	Stunts by the amazing Red Ace bike team
4:30pm	Costume parade
5:00pm	Daring Devils parachute team drop in from the sky
5:45pm	Marching Band

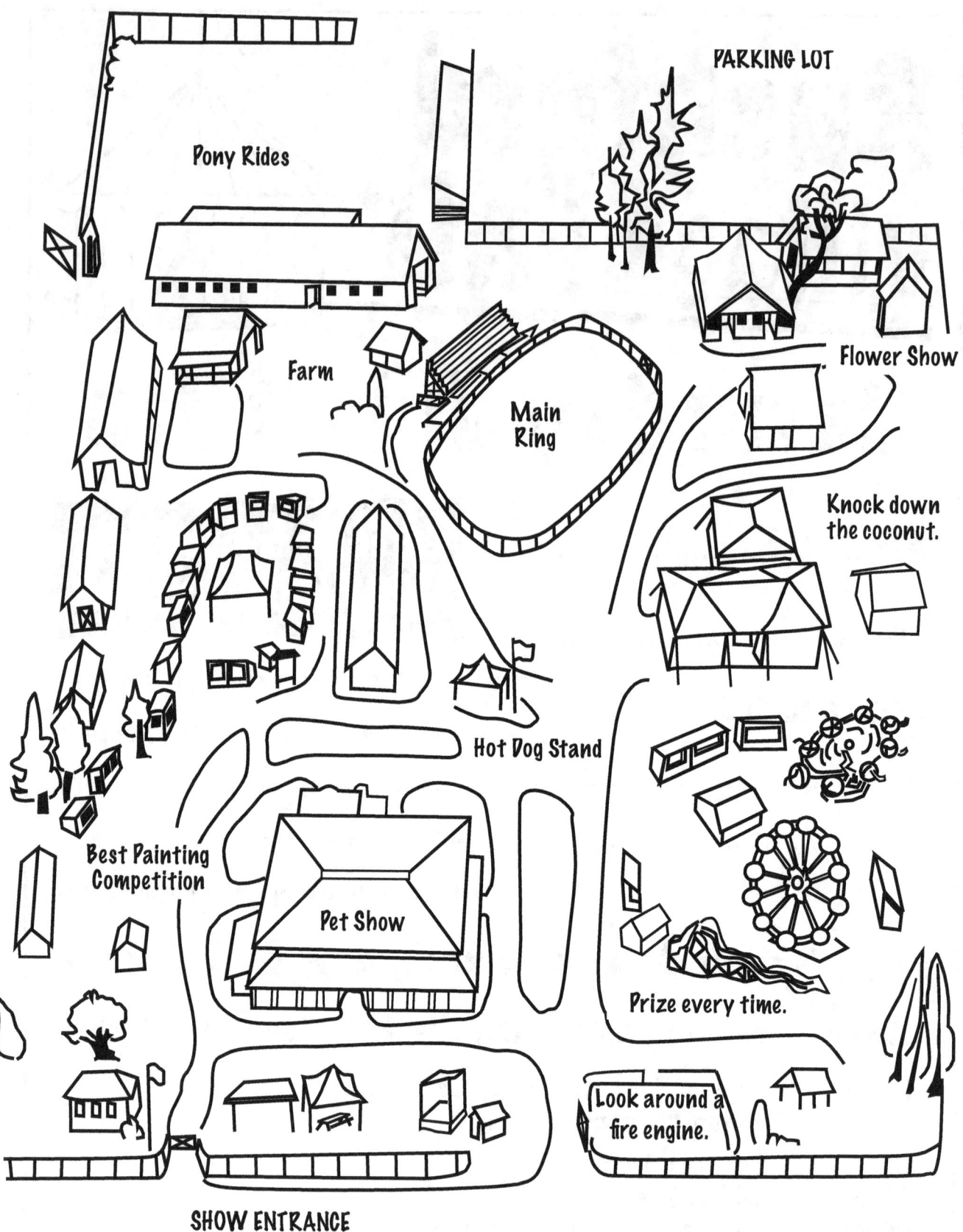

In the main ring the girls and boys of Rushford Dance Academy entertain with their dancing.

At the hot dog stand enjoy juicy hot dogs on grilled rolls, fried crunchy onions and squirts of ketchup.

Draw your own plan.

Exclusive News Today					July 17th 2020

RUSHFORD GAZETTE

All About Rushford

SPECIAL RUSHFORD FAIR EDITION | **HEAT WAVE FOR RUSHFORD'S ANNUAL SUMMER FAIR.**

CROWDS FLOCK TO ANNUAL FAIR

Rushford Fair Draws Record Crowd

By Anya Smith

Picture: Parachutist

The boiling hot sun on Saturday drew thousands of people to the annual Rushford village fair. The whole town turned out.

The Fair, which is always popular, had more stalls than ever. There was an opportunity to buy crafts: hand made jewelry and delicious homemade cakes and jams.

There was a spectacular display from the birds of prey, but a moment of panic, when 'Buzz' refused to come down from a tall tree, despite being tempted down with tasty treats. Bill, a fireman, put his ladder up against the tree to catch the bird, but it flew off. If anyone sees an eagle in their garden, please call the Rushford Bird Sanctuary.

The most exciting moment of the day was the daring stunts from the Red Ace bike team, who thrilled the crowd by leaping over high fences and riding through a ring of fire. Children were warned not to try stunts like this.

The crowd waited with anticipation for the parachutists to drop in. The plane was fifteen minutes late arriving, but the atmosphere in the crowd was so good that nobody minded. There was great excitement when the parachutists started to fall from the sky.

Emma Shaw, aged 13, won the horse jumping competition, with the fastest time in the jump-off on her horse Silver Light. Elijah Mendez came in second.

Becky Smith, aged 6, won the costume competition, dressed as Cindrella. Simon White won second prize, dressed as Aladdin's lamp and Kirk Taylor won third prize as Peter Pan.

Lilly, aged 10, said, "It was the most amazing day out. The atmosphere was great. Everyone was happy. The Rushford Dancers kept everyone entertained with their amazing routines from popular shows."

Finn added, "There were so many good stalls this year. I won loads of prizes."

Mrs. Mcfarlane, 42, added, "It has been excellent. The weather has been on our side."

Laura Jones, 30, commented, "There is such a lovely mix of things. There is everything from food and crafts, through to farm animals and machinery. It's a wonderful two days."

John Saunders, 67, agreed, "We come most years. There is a great family atmosphere and it's a lovely day out."

Catherine Mcdonald, 50, one of the organizers of the show, said, "It is always difficult to say how many people have come through the gates, but I would say we have had record crowds."

This year's show was so popular that we are already planning next year's event.

Facts are *true*

Opinions are what the *writer thinks*

Can you find some facts and opinions in the newspaper article?

Newspaper articles:

- have an exciting headline that grab the reader's attention.

- summarize the event in the first paragraph *(when, who, why, what, where).*

- tell the story in a series of short paragraphs in the order it happened.

- Include quotations from people who were there and a comment from the writer.

- Use direct and reported speech.

   Mrs. Mcfarlane said, "The weather was good."
   Mrs. Mcfarlane said that the weather was good.

Our Trip to Rushford County Fair

Write a newspaper report for the school magazine. Use the information on the next three pages or make up some information of your own.

Where:	Rushford County Showground
When:	8am to 5pm
Why:	to see the show
Who:	Mrs. Barker
What happened:	Masie got lost while we were watching the...
How was the situation resolved:	She was found by the...

What was your favorite thing? What did you enjoy most?

"the cheerleaders who gave a demonstration"	"a robot who entertained the crowds"	"the ice cream"
"the flying planes"	"horse drawn carts"	"the marching band"
"the cooking demonstration"	"the air show by the Army Air Force"	"the stalls selling crafts including bags, jewelry and fashions"
"the horses, rabbits, llamas, pigs, cows, hens and chicks - they were really sweet"	"the stalls selling yummy home made sweets and candy"	"the horse jumping, especially the young children who hurtled around on their Shetland ponies - dashing over hurdles"
"seeing a pig win first prize in the best of breed competition"	"the jousting competition, where the white knight defeated the evil black knight"	"the large display of red and yellow roses at the flower show"

What kind of people do you think made these remarks?

Children, teachers, parents, grandparents, workers...

Circle facts in red and opinions in blue. Which one contains facts or opinions or both?

- "The tents go up a week before the show"
- "I won four prizes."
- "The traffic is usually so heavy that I have to leave for work two hours earlier, to make sure I get there on time."
- "The Red Ace Stunt Bikes were cool."
- "It's thrilling to jump my horses over the big fences."
- "The incredible parachutists jumped from a plane at three thousand feet. They are so brave."
- "It seems the sky is blue and the sun always shines."
- "Mom makes me a costume for the costume parade every year."
- "The roads in Rushford are full of trucks and cars going to the show."
- "The costume parade is such fun because I can dress up as my favorite character."
- "I watched the events in the main ring for three hours."

"Stroking the soft fur of the animals in the Pet Competition is the best part."

"It was quite hot so I had to wear a sun hat and put on lots of sunscreen - but I did enjoy the Popsicles."

"Buying local crafts in the craft tent was enjoyable."

"I enjoyed the glorious weather and the fantastic sunshine. It was the best day ever."

"I loved the flower tent, because there were so many lovely blooms, but the Food and Drink Experience was very popular with the teachers and parent helpers."

"There were crowds of people everywhere browsing through the stalls."

"The catering area was busy so we had to wait in line for drinks."

"There were crowds at the sports village, but I was still able to take part in the rock climbing."

"I was delighted with how it went. The weather was on our side." (Organizer)

"There was such a lovely mix of things, from food and crafts to farm machinery. It was wonderful." (Teacher)

"I would come next year because there was such a lovely atmosphere. It was a lovely day out for everyone."

"I enjoyed saying hello to the friendly goats."

"I enjoyed watching The Sheep Show, where the animals were introduced as if they were stars. Each animal had a name and the sheep man introduced each one in turn.

Then he tried to do a sheep shearing demonstration. He pushed Dolly to the ground and started to shear off her fleece with some electric scissors. She was angry and ran away, but only to the back of the stage. The sheared sheep looked as if it had no clothes on. After this, the sheep man made all the sheep dance by tapping their hooves and nodding their heads to the music."

"There was another man there, with four ferrets, called Slinker, Speedy, Charlie and Ben. He raced them down some tubes. He asked for volunteers to come inside the ring to cheer them on. Some of the boys in our class put their hands up.

After this, there was a sheepdog demonstration. A black and white dog called a Border Collie made some sheep go into a pen."

Eyewitness Account

Write a show story as if you were there.

- Dolly the sheep escapes
- Dogs fight in the dog show
- Animal escapes and eats the best blooms in the flower show
- I knocked over a prize winning exhibit
- Hawk flies away at the Bird of Prey demonstration
- My animal wins 'Best in Show'
- I am a judge in the Best of Breed competition
- Things don't go quite as planned in the...

    You can choose the:
    - terrier racing
    - BMX bike jumping
    - Parachute jumping
    - Motorcycle racing
    - Parade ring

Write a recount about your visit to a show:

Introduction
- Where did you go? (who, when, where, why)
- Recount what happened in several paragraphs.
- Write in detail about anything interesting that happened.
- Comment about things you liked or disliked.

Conclusion
- What did you think at the end of the show?
- Use connectives - finally, after this, next, soon, lastly.

RUSHFORD GAZETTE does a special feature on vacations.

The words of a travel brochure are written persuasively.

Rushford Gazette May 8th 2020

Let's get *away*... where shall we go?

Cruising

Cruising along on a cruise ship is one of the best vacations you can have. Imagine getting away from all the hustle and bustle of the city, to weave your way leisurely along the water. That would be amazing, wouldn't it?

If you choose a vacation afloat, you can book tickets for an international cruise and explore the great oceans. You can choose any destination you like, from the icy waters around Alaska to the warm and sandy beaches of the Caribbean islands.

What will you see? It all depends on which wonderful watery destination you've chosen. You may see icebergs, mountains, and whales if you sail north, or you may sail south and visit a tropical island to see sparkling blue seas, coral reefs, and stunning sunsets.

Get away from all your worries and glide effortlessly along. You could be docking next to a majestic waterfall, or a few steps from a sunny, pretty village that you can explore. Why not spend a warm summer evening having a fruity shake and delicious dinner on your cruise ship, miles from home? How would that feel?

Rushford Gazette May 8th 2020

Let's go on a voyage of...
Discovery,

... around New York City, with NYC Circle Line Cruises. A trip around the city is everything you could wish for, because hardly a minute goes by without a historical building coming into view. You will see the Empire State Building, the tallest building in the city. You will also see the Brooklyn Bridge, which connects Brooklyn and Manhattan. As you near the south tip of Manhattan, the Statue of Liberty will come into view. Along your route, you will also see many other ships and ferries carrying commuters and cargo to our bustling city.

More than this, you can chat to other tourists on the boat as you stop to grab a snack or a drink from our convenient food stand or to use one of the bathrooms which appear on every level of the boat. We do all the work for you so you can enjoy the sights around you. Our helpful guides will share all kinds of historical information during the ride, so you can learn more about New York.

We have been welcoming families and groups from all over the world for over sixty years, many of whom return again and again. Please book a fantastic trip on one of our Circle Line Cruises. Visit www.circleline42.com for more info.

Write to **PERSUADE**

Convince your reader to go somewhere.

- Use good phrases.

    'Imagine getting away from it all'

- Use amazing adjectives and nouns.

    fantastic countryside, delicious food, pretty villages

- Use good verbs.

    You can float, explore, hide

- Use good verbs and adverbs.

    glide effortlessly, explain easily

- Talk directly to your reader.

    you will, you can

- Use bossy verbs or imperatives.

    choose, explore

- Use rhetorical questions that don't need an answer.

    That would be amazing, wouldn't it?

- Use connectives.

    More than this...

Can you find more examples?

Your turn to write a brochure.

> Here are some facts on the **Farm Museum**.
> Let's persuade the reader to go there.

You can find out what life was like in the past...

- how windmills pumped water off the land so farmers could grow things there

You can carry...

- a backpack on your back with a picnic
- binoculars ready to get a closer look at rare birds
- a camera, to capture those picturesque scenes

- **You can see...**

- farmhouses where farmers lived in the past
- a pretty orchard of apple trees
- ponds full of ducks
- quaint barns
- birds like: grebes, herons, ducks and others
- the beehives, where beekeepers collect delicious fresh honey

You can hear...

- bird song
- cows mooing and sheep bleating as they graze in the meadows
- the roar of the wind
- the quacking of ducks in their pond
- the humming of tractors

You can do...

- bird watching
- long walks through the meadows and historical sites
- breathe really fresh country air

STRUCTURE

- Choose some information you would like to include. Use senses; do, see, hear and feel.
- Decide which order you will write about them. Use lists of describing words.
- Now write three paragraphs persuading people to come for a trip here. Use persuasive language.

Come to the FARM MUSEUM

A TRIP YOU WON'T FORGET!

If you want a really relaxing trip, why not come to the Historic Farm Museum. If you don't know, it is situated in New York State, just three hours from the city. It is a vast expanse of farmland, preserved for over a hundred years. It is an ideal place to escape to the country. You can stay in a cottage or bed and breakfast in a pretty town nearby.

More than this, you will be able to find out what it would have been like to live in past times. You will see many crops growing that have been feeding families on the farm for many years. You will see orchards, meadows, barns, and even a modern greenhouse, where certain plants can grow in the warm conditions.

Don't forget your binoculars. You will be able to spot rare birds, ducks, herons and songbirds - as you walk across the farm and around the picturesque land. Imagine strolling along the country paths, with your backpack on your back, listening to the sweet songs of birds. Imagine what it would be like to spot a rare species of bird through your binoculars in the trees around the meadow. Besides this, you will enjoy breathing in the fresh air and feel the wind in your hair. It will certainly be a trip you won't forget.

Make a persuasive tourist brochure for a vacation in Europe. Fold a piece of paper in three. Choose from the notes on the next pages. Write in sentences.

See ....

Eat ....

Visit ....

Come to ....

Get away from it all. Choose a vacation sailing the miles of unspoiled waterways in the Norfolk Broads, outside of London in the UK.	**Things to see:** • charming villages with pretty thatched roof cottages • ancient churches and castles steeped in history • poppies and wildflowers growing along the dykes • rare species of birds and ducks • interesting wildlife • rolling hills and spectacular countryside - from forests to meadows • fields of sheep and cows • a conservation area of unique beauty	**Things to do:** • soak up the sun • weave quietly along the river or canal and admire unspoiled scenery at a leisurely pace • relax and read a book • fish • do bird watching • take photographs • have lunch at a café • enjoy an ice cream at the dock • feed the ducks • watch the sun setting in the evening over the hills
Pass (under) • bridges aquaducts • through locks • stunning scenery	**Words to describe it:** • the river winds (meanders) • the valleys are scattered with villages • the scenery is breathtaking	**How will you feel:** • I feel like I have slipped back in time • peaceful • relaxed • I do not want to go home

Use phrases like...

- Enjoy the vacation of a lifetime...
- If you want a relaxing vacation...
- A vacation that is everything you could wish for...
- One of the best kinds of vacations...
- An amazing vacation that you will never forget...

Choose an action-packed vacation in Holland. Experience the culture of Amsterdam.	**Things to see:** - flat landscape - you can see for miles - pretty villages - historic buildings - medieval opera houses - fields of bulbs like tulips and daffodils (in spring) - windmills dotted along the canals	**Things to do:** - hire a bike and cycle around the city - cruise along a canal - visit an art gallery and see paintings by famous artists like Rembrandt - talk to friendly people - try on clogs - taste delicious Dutch foods like Edam cheese
Visit: - Amsterdam and the amazing sights this city has to offer - a diamond factory where you can see diamond polishing - exhibitions like the Anne Frank museum - climb to the top of a windmill	**How I feel about it:** - Holland has something for everyone - is full of character - step back in time	**Words to describe it:** - unspoiled, charming place - magical - wonderful - colorful - full of history - vibrant - captivating - full of character - peaceful

Choose the Cote d'Azur in the South of France. A relaxing, sun drenched travel destination.

Things to see:
- rugged coast lines
- spectacular views from the cliff top roads
- medieval walled towns and sleepy hill top villages
- wooded valleys cathedrals and ancient chateaux (castles)
- vineyards as far as the eye can see
- fields of golden sunflowers and fragrant lavender
- charming farms
- Roman remains

Things to do:
- stroll through colorful street markets
- visit medieval castles with high towers and dark dungeons
- laze around on sun drenched beaches by the Mediterranean sea
- swim in the crystal clear waters
- see soaring mountains in the distance
- explore mazes of narrow streets
- play a game of horseshoe in the village square
- take a fragrant walk amid fields of lavender

Visit
- The Camargue
- an area of lagoons and marshes near Marseille
- see white galloping horses and
- pink flamingos posing in the midday sun
- have a tour of a perfume factory
- sightsee amongst the Roman remains

Words to describe it:
- bright sun shine
- clear blue sky
- rivers meandering gently through the countryside
- charming mountain villages
- breathtaking views
- calm, quiet, unspoiled
- eat fresh local produce
- soak up the atmosphere
- smell the sweet scent of lavender
- hear the song of the cicada (grasshopper)
- escape the noise of the city

Eat:
- sample delicious French cuisine in a restaurant
- enjoy the excellent world renowned cuisine
- eat cheeses
- garlic
  olive oil
- sit in a street café and sip a cool drink while watching the world go by
- enjoy a picnic of local produce under an olive tree

Choose Venice in Italy. **A beautiful, romantic destination.**	**Things to see:** • magnificent churches and palaces, such as Saint Mark's Basilica • lively squares • interesting shops • listen to live music on the piazza in St. Mark's Square • gaze at the most impressive palace in Venice - Palazzo Ducale • explore Italy's most famous art gallery - Galleria del'Accademia	**Things to do:** • a water city, often called the floating city • crawl on a gondola through the city's maze of narrow waterways • cruise along the Grand Canal and admire the views • watch the world go by from chic cafes • photograph the incredible sites • enjoy sightseeing
Visit • art galleries • museums and churches • walk the ancient winding streets beside the canals • take home souvenirs like Venetian glass, carnival masks and lace and water colors of Venetian scenes	**How I feel about it:** • a unique place • nowhere else like it in the world • Venice captures your imagination • breath taking • steeped in history and culture • like stepping back in time	**Words to describe it:** • full of history • breath taking views • enchanting • wonderful culture and history • a tourist hotspot

> George and Christabelle ask their listeners to phone in, text or email. They have been discussing where they would go and what they would do if they could take off and go anywhere in the world! The most interesting listener will win his or her 'dream' trip.

I would like to dive down into a coral reef in Australia and swim among the colorful tropical fishes.

Please let me ride my horse through the Serengeti Nature Reserve near Mount Kilimanjaro in Tanzania. My horse and I would gallop briskly keeping up with the herds of zebras and gazelles. At dusk, we would watch buffalos and elephants drinking at their waterholes. We would see a pile of bones. My horse would flare his nostrils to warn me if there was a lion close by. We'd gallop away as quickly as we could go.

It is my dream to have husky dogs drag me on a sleigh through the thick snow of the North Pole. Cool!

My dream is to ride a white horse along the beach in Australia, bouncing through the waves and hear him snorting through his nostrils as he steps through the surf.

I would like to plunge through rivers on my mountain bike, zip crazily along the forest tracks and take the bends sideways in a tailspin of dust on an extreme mountain biking vacation.

Give me smoked salmon and fresh prawn sandwiches under a thatched umbrella on a golden beach. The waves would be splashing noisily on the rocks below.

I would like to take the chair lift down a mountain and see the stunning views.

It's out to sea for me. One man on the helm and one to work the deck. We'd haul up the sails of our yacht and ride the waves in the light breeze.

I am 83 but to ride a zip wire across the Grand Canyon as if I was flying would be awesome. I would put my harness on and soon I'd be leaving the ground rapidly. I would see the lake below and fly over the granite cliff, as I zoomed towards the water at 40mph. The view would be awesome... or maybe I would do a parachute jump from a plane....Why not?

I would like to handle lots of different terrains on a mountain bike. I'd get in shape and see lots of beautiful places in the world.

I would just love to trail through the rainforest and clamber through all that tropical vegetation and see monkeys, tropical birds and butterflies. I would catch fish in the river and cook them on a campfire. I would find a tribe in some remote place, talk to the natives and tell them about the modern world. It would be a once in a lifetime trip.

I just love history so I would take a trip to Egypt. I would take a camel ride across the desert and see the pyramids: one of the 'seven wonders of the world.'

What destination would you choose if you could visit anywhere in the world?

Imagine these dreams come true for the listeners and write the stories.

I need to get in shape, so I'd like a nice easy walking trip, across an amazing city like Sydney. I'd need a pair of tough, designer sneakers to propel my feet along, as I pass all the sites, like the opera house and the suspension bridge. As the finishing line comes into sight I'd have a big spurt of energy.

I would climb a tall mountain with a guide. I would have a team of donkeys carrying my backpacks. From the top I would see amazing views. It would be incredible.

Use the questions to write about a vacation that you enjoyed.

- Where did you go?

- Did you have time off school or did you go away on a school trip?

- How did you get there? (plane, boat, car)

- Was the weather hot on your vacation?

- Where did you stay?

- What was the (hotel, apartment, cottage, caravan) like?

- What did you do on your vacation?

- Did you swim, ride a horse, walk, play games or visit places?

- What event did you enjoy most on your vacation?

- Do you have any more special memories:

    - of the places you visited
    - of the things you saw?

- Did you bring any souvenirs home?

- Would you like to go to the same place again?

- Why?

Read these facts.

Over five hundred years ago in 1492, there was a famous Italian sailor called Christopher Columbus, who set out on a voyage to reach his dream destination.

In those days, sailors had only traveled east as far as China. Christopher Columbus knew that the world was round. He had a dream that he could find a new sea route by sailing in the opposite direction of the one taken by other explorers, by sailing west towards Asia and the Spice Islands.

He told the Queen of Spain, Isabella, that his voyage would take two weeks. Queen Isabella wanted to do trade with these new places. If Columbus could reach these new lands, he could bring back rich cargoes of silks, spices and other luxurious eastern goods, so she agreed to pay for it and he set sail in his three boats, The Santa Maria, The Nina and The Pinta.

For nearly four months, they sailed west across the seas, but they did not come to land. Sometimes it was calm at sea and they sailed under a starry sky. Then the sky grew dark grey and thunder roared loudly. The wind tossed the boat up and down on the waves. The sailors were so scared that their ship would sink, that they started shouting angrily.

Then Christopher kneeled down and prayed to God that they might come to land. His crew were threatening to mutiny, (to fight between themselves) so he thought he would have to go back. Then, he saw something in the distance that warmed his heart. It was land. He shouted 'Land! Land!' He had discovered the Caribbean Islands (the Americas), but he thought he had discovered Asia. His ships landed on an island in The Bahamas. He claimed the islands for the King and Queen of Spain. His discovery led to Europeans settling in The Americas.

Write down some facts about Christopher Columbus.

-
-
-

Write an extract from the diary of Christopher Columbus.

Day 1: We set sail from Spain. We are sailing West ....
....
Day 2: ....
....
....

Write a newspaper report about Christopher Columbus dated 1492.

Make a list of **sea words**.

- stormy
- giant waves
- lashing
- splashing
- hitting
- rocking
- tossing
- turning
- ....
- ....
- ....

Comprehension Test   What facts did you find out?

1. Where was Christopher Columbus born?
2. When did he live?
3. What was his job?
4. What were the names of his ships?
5. Which queen did he ask to pay for the expedition?
6. Why did she agree?
7. How many weeks did the ship sail with no sight of land?
8. How did the sailors feel? Why?
9. How did Christopher Columbus act when his crew were angry?
10. What changed this?

Circle the correct answer

1. Columbus set sail in August 1750

   1492

   1950.

2. He landed in San Salvador on 12th October 1492

   1836

   1996.

3. People did not know that America existed at that time.

   People regularly traveled to the USA at that time.

4. Columbus sailed in a wooden sailing boat.

   Columbus sailed in a powerful motorboat.

   Columbus wanted silks, jewels and spices from the east.

5. The conditions were bad for the forty sailors on board.

   Food was kept in freezers on the boat.

   There wasn't much room to store food.

   The boat was huge.

True or False?

6. The people living on the Caribbean Islands were known as Indians (because early explorers thought they were in India.)

7. Some people thought the world was flat and that you might fall off the edge of it.

Name some explorers?

Can you match these explorers to the lands they explored? Find out some more facts about each one. Use the web or an encyclopaedia.

Captain James Cook   Marco Polo   Roald Amundsen

Captain Robert Scott   Hernando Cortes   Francisco Pizarro
Frances

Now match each explorer to his expedition.

- He sailed in a ship called 'The Endeavour' with 112 sailors and became the first European to visit New Zealand and the east coat of Australia.

- A Norwegian sailor, who led a team to The South Pole in 1912, beating a team of British explorers.

- An Italian explorer from Venice, who discovered the great civilization of China and who became a favorite with Kublai Khan, the Mongol ruler.

- He sailed on a ship called 'The Discovery,' to within 900 miles of the South Pole, but he was beaten by an explorer from another country.

- He conquered the Incas of Peru in South America and marched into Peru with 200 soldiers. He was hungry for gold, silver and land.

- In 1519 he set out from Cuba to conquer the Aztecs of Mexico.

Grade Six is writing a play. Can you help them finish it?

Scene 1

Captain:	Your Majesty I have a dream that there are new lands to be explored. I will take a ship and travel east.
Queen:	But, what if you fall off the edge of the world?
Captain:	I believe the world is round.
Queen:	What will my country get out of this?
Captain:	You will be able to trade with these countries. They will have cargoes of silks and spices.
Queen:	In that case, I will pay for the voyage.

Continue the play script.

Scene 2 *(On the boat)*

Sailors are angry	We've been sailing for nearly 4 months and there is no sight of land.
Captain:	Give me a few more days.
1st mate:	No, you brought us on a dangerous voyage.
2nd mate:	Look! The sky is black. We're in for another storm.

Continue the play script.

Scene 3

1st mate:	Ah Help! Oh No.
	The ship is rocking. We're done for!
2nd mate:	The ship is going to go down. We'll all die!
	(Christopher Columbus knelt down and prayed to God.)

Continue the play script.

Scene 4

Captain:	Oh God. What is going to happen to us? Help us. Please help us.
Crew:	Throw him overboard. He's trying to drown us.
1st mate:	Yes, I think we ought to throw him over board.
Captain:	Please, please make the wind stop. Save us.
Jim: *(on the mast)*	What's that ahead? It looks like land. Thank God. We've reached land.

Continue the play script.

Scene 5

Queen: What have you here?

Captain: Silk and spices.

Town Crier: I announce that this day, Christopher Columbus, has pleased the queen by discovering the Americas.

Continue the play script.

Write some more dialogue for each scene in the play.

Do you think the play script makes the characters more real?

What props and sound effects would you need to show the setting of the play?

Think of some other ways a play script entertains the audience.

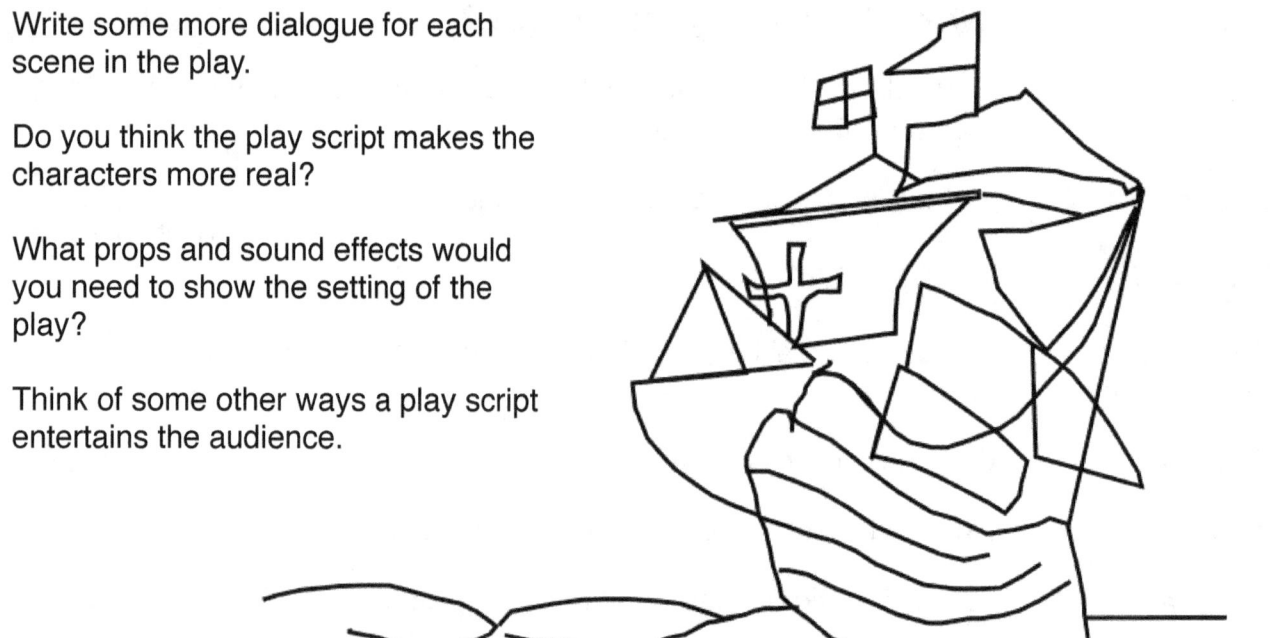

Characters

Queen Isabella
Captain Columbus
1st Mate
2nd Mate
Jim
Town Crier

Setting

Scene 1: A palace in Spain

Scene 2: On the Ocean

Try writing a play script about an explorer. Use the internet to help you.

Now research some favorite vacation destinations in the world. Use the internet or an encyclopaedia to find information. Collect some travel brochures from the travel agent. Collect words and phrases. Make a brochure. Choose from:

Japan	Seychelles	Hawaii	Australia
California	Philippines	Fiji	Florida
Jamaica	Kenyan Safari	Florence	Venice
France	Thailand	Tahiti	Bahamas
India	China		

The **WONDERS** of the *World*

Match the wonder to the country.

Great Wall of China	Egypt
Petra	India
Christ the Redeemer	Mexico
Machu Picchu	Italy
Chichen Itza	Jordan
Colosseum	Brazil
Taj Mahal	Peru
Great Pyramid of Giza	China

Find some facts out about each wonder.

Guinea Pig Education can help you use **punctuation** in *your* writing.

Let's get going!

First, don't forget to **write in sentences**. Use **capital letters** and **periods**.

Jules belongs to **S**ydney at 12 **O**live **G**rove, **R**ushford.

Now try this one:

lois and lulu belong to anya at 14 chesterfield gardens rushford

---

Use a **!**

That's exciting!
What a surprise!
Oh bother!

Use a **?**

What do guinea pigs eat?

Hold out a piece of vegetable. Will your guinea pig eat it?

Now try this one:

guinea pigs like to be stroked do they bite they are timid but rarely bite ouch

---

Do not forget to use "**.....**" when you use **direct speech**.

"Anya, what did you buy at the pet shop?" said Jules.
"I bought a cage, some straw, some hay, a bowl, a water bottle and some food for my new guinea pigs."

Use commas for **Lists**.

Use commas **before or after** a **phrase** or subordinate **clause** in a sentence.

Use commas **around a clause hidden** in the **middle of a complex sentence**.

Try these:

Lois is lively inquisitive and nosy
Guinea pigs can be chocolate black silver white and tortoise shell.
My guinea pig called Jules has long hair.
After cleaning the cage Anya put in some hay.

Try these: *(answers on next page)*

What is your guinea pig like anya

Lulu has a white coat, uneven colored spots and black ears she replied

After running in the grass Jules dozed in his hutch.

Guinea Pigs in the wild live in a burrow.

Some guinea pigs with long hair have rosettes.

Let's remember **apostrophes**:

The carrot belonging to Jules is **Jules's carrot.**

The hutch of Lois and Lulu is the **guinea pigs' hutch.**

Plus, remember apostrophes for shortened words.

They are gorgeous.
They're gorgeous.

For extra information you may need to use a **dash** for a longer pause.

Dad bought Anya a guinea pig - it was so sweet.

Jules nibbled his carrot loudly - crunch, crunch, crunch.

Or you could use **parentheses** for extra information.

The guinea pigs (Lois and Lulu) scampered across the grass.

Try these:

The guinea pig belongs to Kate.

The hutch of the rabbits George and Ginger.

Isnt he sweet.

Try these:

Anya fed her guinea pig he was hungry.

The rabbits George and Ginger are great friends.

How did you do?

- Lois and Lulu belong to Anya at 14 Chesterfield Gardens, Rushford.
- Guinea pigs like to be stroked. Do they bite? They are timid but rarely bite. Ouch!
- Lois is lively, inquisitive and nosy.
- Guinea pigs can be chocolate, black, silver, white and tortoise shell.
- My guinea pig, called Jules, has long hair.
- After cleaning the cage, Anya put in some hay.
- "What is your guinea pig like Anya?"
  "Lulu has a white coat, uneven colored spots and black ears," she replied.
- After running in the grass, Jules dozed in his hutch.
- Guinea pigs, in the wild, live in a burrow.
- Some guinea pigs, with long hair, have rosettes.
- Kate's guinea pig/ the rabbits' hutch/ Isn't he sweet.
- Anya fed her guinea pig - he was hungry.
- The rabbits (George and Ginger) are great friends.
- The male guinea pig is a boar; the female is a sow.

Finally, you can use a **colon** in a list.

Jess had five smart guinea pigs: a short haired coat, a long coarse coat, a deep shining coat, a smooth coat and one with rosettes and twirls.

Or you can use a **semicolon** to separate two similar ideas in a list.

Guinea pigs are sociable; they like company.

Try this:
The male guinea pig is a boar the female is a sow.

Make a sentence with a :
Make a sentence with a ;

Aren't I sweet?

Of course!

Guinea Pig **Spelling** *Tips*

Guinea pig says, "Don't forget it is important to read through your writing, so you can spot any obvious mistakes. Here are a few basic spelling tips. Make sure you can spell all the words on these pages."

Tricky homophones

Homophones sound the same but are spelled differently.

*I gave **two** carrots **to** Jules but he's getting **too** fat.*

***Our** guinea pigs **are** cute.*

*They're over **there** by **their** hutch.*

Difficult Endings

Some words have tricky endings.

*The **latch** on Jules's **hutch** comes open. He gets out and eats a **patch** of grass by the **hedge**. I try to **catch** him but he **dodges** me and runs off.*

*When I **handle** my little piggy, I **cuddle** him.*

Some words have spelling rules.

You double the final letter of a verb with a short sound.

*I **hug** Jules.
I am **hugging** him.*

*I **pat** the rabbit.
I am **patting** him.*

*I **grab** him.
I am **grabbing** hold of him.*

*He **hops**.
He is **hopping**.*

If the final letter is a consonant, just add the ending.

*He **licks**.
He is **licking**.*

*He **fights**.
He is **fighting**.*

*I **hold** him.
I am **holding** him.*

Drop the 'e' if you are adding an ending with a vowel.

*I **love** my guinea pig.
I am **loving** him.*

*I **stroke** my guinea pig.
I am **stroking** him.*

*He is having an **adventure**.
He is **adventurous**.*

Use the same rule for:

shine   shiny
noise   noisy

But, if the ending begins with a consonant you keep the 'e':

live   lively

love   lovely

lone   lonely

safe   safely

When you add an ending some words change the 'y' to an 'i':

*My guinea pig is **happy**.
He is **happier**.
He is the **happiest**.*

busy   busier   busiest
cry   cries   cried
piggy   piggies
carry   carries   carried

	Comparative	Superlative
He is fast.	faster	the fastest
He is fine.	finer	the finest
He is a beauty.	more beautiful	most beautiful

Use Sounds

ch, sh, wh, th, oo, ee, ar, or, ur, ir, er, e, ai, ay, oi, oy, oa, ow, ou, au, aw, ce, ci, cy, ge, gi, gy, short y, long y, magic e...

... to sound out 80% of words.

Use syllables to sound out hard words.

Eat **VEG ET ABLES**
Soft 'g' - ge, gi, gy.

are **COM FORT ABLE**

like **MIX TURE**

have an **AD VEN TURE**

SEV EN

PRECIOUS

CREATURE

Remember:

1. Sound hard words out using syllables.

2. Jot down words you find difficult. Learn them.

3. Use a dictionary or thesaurus.

Don't forget to keep your writing neat. Small letters should be the same height. There should be one little finger space between each word.

Make sure you can write this passage:

My guinea pigs feed on green leaves. They munch, crunch, scratch, scrunch in their hutch. Early in the morning it is necessary to feed them healthy food and fill up the water container. My noisy young pigs enjoy playing excitedly in their run on the lawn, where they are safe from danger.

Really tricky ones:

'i' before 'e' except after 'c' - when the sound is ee.

believe

fierce

field

conceited

Exceptions:

neighbor

Silent Letters:

Guinea Pigs:

gnaw

clim**b**

eat crum**b**s

are caut**i**ous

are ca**l**m

are **k**nowing

wrinkle up their noses

Tricky words:

Are you **tough enough** to keep a guinea pig?

They can't be **caught**.

They fill one with **laughter**.

They love to be **photographed**.

Guinea pig says, "Make lists of tricky words you find difficult from the groups of words."

The glossary

A starting point:	is something that gives you an idea to write a story.
The genre is:	the type of story you choose to write. It could be a traditional tale that has a message that good overcomes evil or a romance, horror, fantasy, mystery, realistic or adventure story.
Planning a story:	Structuring the story into three or more paragraphs – with a beginning, a middle and an ending.
Characters:	are people who feature in the story – we learn how they behave and about their feelings, motives, emotions and conflicts.
A setting:	is the place where the story takes place - creating a mood.
The Plot:	is a sequence of events that make up the story. Action in the story may be triggered by a conflict, complication, problem, or unexpected event that needs to be solved.
Suspense:	is built up to leave the reader guessing what will happen. Use: • short sentences for impact – 'Help!' • show the feelings of the characters – 'suddenly his heart missed a beat' – to build up a dramatic climax that leaves the reader on the edge of his chair wondering how it will end.
First person:	tells the story, using 'I' or 'we' – so the reader can imagine being the main character.
Second person:	uses 'you' and speaks directly to the reader or involves the reader.
Third person:	uses 'he,' 'she,' 'it,' 'they' to tell the story as a narrator, like a fly on the wall watching.
Atmosphere:	is the mood and feeling conjured up in the story.
Flashback:	if you start your story with action, you may include few details about what went on before.
Ending or resolution:	may be happy, sad, moral (a lesson learned) or a cliffhanger - where the reader imagines his or her own ending.

Paragraphs:	start a new line (one finger space in for handwriting). Use a new paragraph if you change event, time or place.
Conjunctions:	are linking words that start paragraphs or join sentences. Examples are: as, since, because, but, if, then, so, as a result of, for instance, yet, after a while, suddenly.
Dialogue:	is what people say and can move the story on. Use correct punctuation – *Lilly said, "Is it hot in here?"* (direct speech); *Lilly said that it was hot in here.* (indirect or reported speech)
The opening:	is the first sentence of a story - fiction or narrative.
A topic sentence:	is the first sentence in a paragraph, which tells the reader what it will be about. Further sentences will develop the idea and explain it.
Describe:	is making a word picture.
Adjective and noun:	*shimmering sand* (describing word, naming word)
Verb and adverb:	*shouting noisily* (action word, describes action word)
Powerful verbs and adverbs:	Choosing key words – *'a voice sounded mysteriously,' 'he nodded his head anxiously.'*
Similes:	compare using as and like – *'as white as snow'*
Metaphors:	compare two similar things, but don't use like or as. *'The dog was a little monster.'*
Script:	tells a story through the characters' dialogue.
Writers' techniques	include: 　* repetition 　* rhetorical questions - questions that don't need an answer 　* personification - giving an object human qualities 　* onomatopoeia - words that sound like their name 　* alliteration - several words that start with the same letter
Fiction:	includes story and narrative.
Non-fiction:	includes information, diaries, leaflets, reports, recounts, descriptions.
Purpose:	why it is written – to inform, explain, describe, persuade, advise or argue.
Target audience:	are the people the article is written for – to instruct someone on how to use a …, to explain how to get somewhere, to persuade or convince the reader to do something.

www.ingramcontent.com/pod-product-compliance
Lightning Source LLC
Chambersburg PA
CBHW050714090526
44587CB00019B/3381